FORBIDDEN
MATTER

FORBIDDEN MATTER

Religion in the Drama of Shakespeare and His Contemporaries

Gerald M. Pinciss

DELAWARE

Newark: University of Delaware Press
London: Associated University Presses

Associated University Presses
440 Forsgate Drive
Cranbury, NJ 08512

Associated University Presses
16 Barter Street
London WC1A 2AH, England

Associated University Presses
P.O. Box 338, Port Credit
Mississauga, Ontario
Canada L5G 4L8

The paper used in this publication meets the requirements of the American National Standard for Permanence of Paper for Printed Library Materials Z39.48-1984.

Library of Congress Cataloging-in-Publication Data

Pinciss, G. M.
  Forbidden matter : religion in the drama of Shakespeare and his contemporaries / Gerald M. Pinciss.
    p.   cm.
  Includes bibliographical references (p.   ) and index.
  ISBN 0-87413-706-3 (alk. paper)
  1. English drama—Early modern and Elizabethan, 1500–1600—History and criticism.   2. Christianity and literature—England—History—16th century.   3. Christianity and literature—England—History—17th century.   4. English drama—17th century—History and criticism.   5. Christian drama, English—History and criticism. 6. Shakespeare, William, 1564–1616—Contemporaries.   7. Shakespeare, William, 1564–1616—Religion.   8. Religion and literature.
  I. Title.
PR658.R43P56   2000
822'.3093823—dc21   99-38700
                                                                CIP

For
Lewis W. Falb

Utrumque nostrum incredibili modo
        consentit astrum
                —Horace *Odes* Book II, Ode 17

CONTENTS

Acknowledgments

If circumstances lead me I will find
Where truth is hid, though it were hid indeed
Within the centre.

—Hamlet II.ii.

EARLY DRAFTS OF SEVERAL SECTIONS OF THIS BOOK HAVE AP-
peared either as articles or conference papers. In slightly altered
form, parts of the chapters on *Dr. Faustus, Measure for Measure*,
and *Bartholomew Fair* were printed by *Studies in English Literature* in the Spring issues of 1993, 1990, and 1995 respectively.
The discussion of *Measure for Measure* and the Saints' Life Play
was given as a paper at the Shakespeare Association of America
meeting in Chicago, 1995. The chapter on *Perkin Warbeck*, first
heard at the Third International Conference on "History, Politics, and Interpretation, 1520–1660" at the University of Reading, England in July 1995, was presented in an expanded form
at the Columbia University Shakespeare Seminar in September
1996. I am grateful to the editors and publishers who not only
accepted my work but also granted me permission to reprint material that first appeared in their pages. And I am indebted to
them, to their editorial boards, and to organizers and partici-
pants at public meetings where I delivered papers for valuable
and illuminating comments. In addition, I am most appreciative
of the words of encouragement offered by several whose scholarship has been invaluable; in particular, I owe thanks to David
Bevington, Ian Donaldson, R. A. Foakes, Douglas Peterson,
Frances Teague, and Eugene Waith.

For generous help and unfailing patience I was fortunate to
have as colleagues Professors Irene Dash, Calvin Edwards, and
Mildred Kuner, who read installments of my work and offered
astute criticism. Indeed, Professor Dash read my writing more
than once with unflagging attention and intelligence, surely a test

both of her powers of concentration and of her friendship. My former colleague and collaborator, Professor Marlies Danziger, as always, was an ever-reliable friend and advisor; I alone know how much I have profited from her good sense and generosity. And I am especially appreciative of the counsel and wisdom of my collaborator on *Shakespeare's World*, Roger Lockyer. He has acted as my guide through the intricacies of the religious controversy of the period, through the trail of recusants at Harrow, and through the maze of complications that was the Thirty Years' War. For his advice, for his ever-useful suggestions, for his patience, and especially for his friendship I count myself most fortunate. The faults of omission and commission that remain herein are entirely my own.

The dedication acknowledges my greatest indebtedness—and the one for which I am grateful above all.

FORBIDDEN MATTER

1

Introduction:
Religion and Stage Censorship

WHEN EDMUND TILNEY, THE MASTER OF THE REVELS, OR-
dered the writers of the play of *Sir Thomas More* to revise their
script according to his instructions, he ended with the direct
threat: "otherwise att your own perrilles."[1] The words are surely
forbidding. The Revels Office was exercising the power given it
by the Privy Council to prohibit the acting companies, in the
words of the 1598 minutes, to "handle in their plaies certen matters of Divinytie and of State unfitt to be suffred."[2]

But the language of these Star Chamber proceedings does not
forbid *all* matters of divinity and state. Although "censorship
was considerable," it could not be absolute.[3] Moreover, as Stephen Greenblatt points out:

> The Tudor and Stuart regulations governing the public stage were
> confused, inconsistent, and haphazard, the products neither of a tra-
> ditional, collective understanding nor of a coherent, rational attempt
> to regularize and define a new cultural practice. They were instead a
> jumble of traditional rules and offices designed to govern older, very
> different theatrical practices and a set of ordinances drawn up very
> hastily in response to particular and local pressures.[4]

Faced with these inconsistencies, playwrights and revels officers clearly worked out a modus operandi: "conventions that
both sides accepted as to how far a writer could go in explicit address to the contentious issues of his day, how he could encode
his opinions so that nobody would be *required* to make an example of him."[5] As a result the theater managed with considerable
success to discuss forbidden subjects and to dramatize controversial matters despite nominal government prohibitions.[6] As

13

Samuel Calvert wrote to Sir Ralph Winwood in March 1605, "The Players do not forbear to present upon their Stage the whole Course of this present Time not sparing either King, State or Religion, in so great Absurdity, and with such Liberty, that any would be afraid to hear them."[7]

It is hardly surprising that religion ranked with politics as an especially sensitive topic in post-Reformation England; they were hardly separable. Moreover, matters of faith involved deep convictions, often accompanied by very strong emotions. After all, how one spent eternity was at stake! And religious allegiances among the citizenry varied greatly. Those in the Church of England accepted the Elizabethan compromise and the Thirty-Nine Articles, which left open the possibility that all were eligible for salvation. Calvinists, however, believed that Christ died only for those singled out for salvation so that all others not so "elected" are "reprobated to damnation." Presbyters were intent on reforming the administrative structure of the church, and the "hotter Protestants" argued with intense fervor on the need to purify the English Church of all remnants of Catholicism.[8] Finally, there were those in the population who were still Catholics, some holding their political loyalty to England, others to Rome. And in each of these groups the devout were prepared to argue with all the fanaticism of zealots and bigots.

Since it was such a sensitive subject, religion was "the topic above all on which successive monarchs and their Councils wished to suppress comment;" and so the Revels Office was established, as Richard Dutton notes in what is the most recent, thorough study of this organization.[9] The government responded by setting up controls—bureaucratic mechanisms for preventing the performances and the printing of play texts it deemed dangerous. The office of the master of the revels, a court appointee, was expanded, and that functionary was authorized to license all scripts, signifying the approval necessary for performance. To soothe the complaints of the clergy and the city, the Privy Council agreed to the appointment of two "men of learning and judgment," one chosen by the archbishop of Canterbury and the other by the lord mayor of London, to join with the master of the revels to "stryke out or reforme suche partes and matters as they shall fynde unfitt and undecent to be handled in playes, bothe for Divinitie and State."[10] Yet the master of the revels seems to have continued as independently as before, despite the persistent complaints from members of the church and from the governing authorities of the city. Their unhappiness, according to Dutton, is proof that in its functioning, the Revels Office was "a good deal more liberal than it is sometimes given credit for being. . . . One can only conclude that the expression of heterodox, or at least provocative opinions was not in itself grounds for censorship or restraint."[11] Comment on religious issues could not be altogether excluded even though the Crown may have wished it: court factions guarded their particular interests just as the patronage system lent support to particular writers and views, and to avoid charges of excessive partisanship, the master of the revels had to be responsive to all of these. In short, a range of unorthodox or challenging opinions could be aired in the theater so long as these were "properly licensed, suitably veiled and not slanted with offensive particularity at a powerful constituency."[12]

A subject of such intense interest as religion was ideal for treatment in the playhouses—even when one might need to serve it up in a veiled or encoded form—since, both by their shock value and their topicality, plays on religious matters could attract an audience to the theater. Such material, then, would appeal to the commercial interests of the acting companies, and as a consequence many playwrights were tempted to write about religion. And since differences among religious beliefs could provide the kinds of conflicts necessary for drama, even playwrights with unexceptionable religious opinions found it of practical value. Moreover, since players, traveling widely and performing before a varied audience, could broadly disseminate the biases of their repertory, even those who most certainly did not like the theater could find it useful for their own purposes. The geographical range of touring companies and the diverse audiences who came to see them were no small advantages in an age with limited means of attaining widespread communication. In the playhouses, at least, even illiteracy was not an obstacle.

For their part, the monarchs and their counselors also appreciated the value of the theater, despite its dangers. Seldom were the playhouses shut down by the court and, except on very rare occasions, not for very long. After all, the theater could be used to disseminate the dominant ideology even as it was liable to subversive appropriation. As Jean Howard has pointed out:

To say . . . that the state and the theater were not coextensive and that the material circumstances of theatrical writing and theatrical production created conditions for ideological contest and contradiction, does not mean that Elizabethan drama was inherently subversive, simply that its implication in the mediation of social conflict and in the reproduction of dominant ideologies was often strongly marked by contradictions and fissures, and the outcome of its recuperative strategies always uncertain.[13]

Experienced politicians understood not only that repression can never be complete but also that it might prove far more dangerous than controlled expression. They therefore agreed to pursue what has been called a policy of containment, letting their agents "geve allowance of suche [playscripts] as they shall thincke meete to be plaied and to forbydd the rest."[14]

In effect, the approval of the master of the revels protected plays from the far more stringent controls desired by the authorities of church and state. Ironically, this tension between the wishes of the church and city on the one hand and the will of the court and council on the other served the best interests of the theater, for these competing pressure groups forced the court and council to be perhaps more liberal than they would have been otherwise. With all of these rival interests it is no wonder, as Richard Burt observes, that "the court's model of theatrical legitimation was contradictory to the point of incoherence."[15] More important for us was an unanticipated benefit of this situation: it encouraged the writing of subtle and complex playscripts, "suitably veiled," to use Richard Dutton's phrase, or "signaling according to cautious codes," to quote Martin Butler.[16]

To survive, the theater had to appeal to a larger public and attract a diverse audience by touching on issues that were under examination, unresolved and controversial. In Alan Sinfield's words, theater

was the mode of cultural production in which market forces were strongest, and as such it was especially exposed to the influence of subordinate and emergent classes. We should not, therefore, expect any straightforward relationship between plays and ideology: on the contrary, it is even likely that the topics that engaged writers and audiences alike were those where ideology was under strain.[17]

Encoded discussion of such a controversial subject as religion was the only recourse, and this required subtlety, complexity, and enrichment of the material. Dramatic literature was born of necessity.

This book examines some half dozen plays, written between the early 1590s and the early 1630s, that involve the religious controversy of their time. Included in this study are examples from Christopher Marlowe, whose writing initiated the great age of Renaissance drama, to John Ford, whose work appeared at its close. With the exception of the chapter on plays by Heywood and Rowley, the works under consideration here have long been appreciated; they are highly regarded as literature and often studied as representative of the achievement and variety of the English Renaissance theater. Although their fame and reputation are deserved, I hope to show that at least for their first audiences, they were a great deal more than entertainment.

Each of the chapters that follows will consider a different type of play and the devices used to take up a nominally forbidden subject; that is, the means by which each playwright commented on some aspect of the religious controversy without endangering the viability of his work. The examples have been chosen in most cases not only for their literary merit but also for the variety of their genres; tragedy, "problem play," quasi-historical pageant, comedy, and chronicle history are all represented. Even more important, each of these works expresses a different view on issues relating to religion. In some cases, such as *Dr. Faustus*, religion is in the foreground of the action and dramatized as a personal issue; in others, such as *Bartholomew Fair* and *Perkin Warbeck*, religion is a tangential but nevertheless crucial issue related to matters of contemporary politics.

Of the works that we shall consider, surely Marlowe's *Doctor Faustus* is the most explicitly concerned with religion. Its hero rejects Christianity, sells his soul to the devil and ends by being dragged off to hell. Good and Evil Angels prompt him, instructing him and us on the joys and sorrows that attend his actions. In addition, lest we mistake the message, a chorus offers a prologue and epilogue commenting on the life and death of a willful sinner for our moral benefit. How could the authorities object to all this? What could be more acceptable to the orthodox position of the Church of England? Yet, as we shall see, the sectarian lesson of the play is impossible to determine with any assurance. Is the world of *Doctor Faustus* one that conforms to the teaching of the Church of England or one in which a Calvinist deity exercises his inscrutable will? In short, was Faustus damned because of the choices he made, or did he choose as he did because he was damned at birth, a reprobate? We shall find only equivocation in the play, for it comes near to contradicting itself at crucial moments, maintaining by a delicate balance the opposing explanations for the hero's motives.[18] And while this struggle between the two most hotly argued Protestant positions is played out, the story is heightened by the thrill of wonders enacted through forbidden magic and by the dazzle of its poetry, a music unheard in blank verse before Marlowe. For all of these reasons Marlowe's play holds a place unique on the English stage for its longevity and influence.

In *Measure for Measure*, called his "most theological play," Shakespeare dramatizes religious questions by presenting them through even more complex devices than Marlowe employed in *Doctor Faustus*.[19] In Shakespeare's work, all the paradigms of the medieval saints' life play are suggested through the three principal characters: Isabella appears as the tested martyr; Angelo, the repentant sinner; and the Duke, the disguised holy agent. But in each case these paradigms are deconstructed either by the psychological complexity of the characters that denies them the purity and single-mindedness typical of truly saintly motivation; or by unexpected turns in the plot; or even by supporting roles, such as the slanderer Lucio's, that undermine the conventional reading. Moreover, the deconstructed Catholic paradigm that evolves out of character is matched by an ambivalently treated Protestant theme that evolves out of a repeated action: how positive are the effects of the despair felt when confronting one's immediate death or the immediate death of those close to us? The question is hardly an idle one, for belief in what the Duke calls the "heavenly comforts of despair" was a contested matter among Catholic, Church of England, and Calvinist worshipers. All of these discussed with varying degrees of conviction the paradoxical notion that positive effects can result from temporarily doubting God's love, and this is indeed what Shakespeare has dramatized, leaving the notion problematic.

There is little problematic, however, about the religious faith of the playwrights discussed in the next chapter, for the two plays considered there, Samuel Rowley's *When You See Me You Know Me* and Thomas Heywood's *If You Know Not Me You Know Nobody*, are far clearer in their sympathies. One need not doubt that they align themselves squarely with the Church of England in its most rigorously anti-Catholic attitude. Although in their subject matter they are concerned with the reigns of Henry VIII and Elizabeth, their appearance on the stage during the very first years of the Stuart dynasty suggests that they were responding to the behavior of the royal couple, indirectly criticizing the policies and practices of both James and Anne. Yet, since the action of both works strongly endorses accepted, orthodox views of the Church of England, neither play is objectionable even though their very orthodoxy implies a critique of the court's domestic and foreign policy.

The conservative views and crude writing of Heywood and Rowley stand in sharp contrast to the liberal attitude and sophisticated dramaturgy of Ben Jonson in *Bartholomew Fair*. In this work, with an uncharacteristic lightness of touch, Jonson asks Catholics, members of the Church of England, and Puritans what "warrant" they hold for believing they alone are sanctified. Indeed, in the course of the action, representatives of each of these religious positions are set side by side in the stocks, and a character named Grace has to find her salvation not through the dogma of a particular religion but through providential intercession. Jonson, it seems, has the temerity to suggest that since no claimant for a particular religious calling can establish absolute righteousness, none should demand dominance or exclusivity.

Knowing that the educated members of his audience were alert to subtle methods of communicating, Jonson could express such a radical thought by following Polonius's advice: "with windlasses and with assays of bias,/ By indirections find directions out." As Annabel Patterson points out, Jonson's "contemporaries were far more sophisticated about the problems of interpretation than we might suppose."[20] Not explicitly but only by allusion and suggestion, by hints and indirect signals, Jonson alerts his audience's attention to a way of decoding his action and reading it. For example, he emphasizes the seemingly irrelevant fact that Bartholomew Cokes makes his home at Harrow on the Hill; and since that location was long associated with Catholic recusants, Bartholomew's religious affiliations might well be identified by his place of residence. In the same way, the associations of Smithfield, the location of Bartholomew Fair, as the site for the burning of Protestants at one time and of Catholics at another, suggests that a modus vivendi would be desirable. Significantly, the name given to Adam Overdo, the justice of the peace who is the central figure of the play, implies that in his fallible humanity he is foolishly excessive as well as that religious tolerance is long "overdue."

The final chapter examines a chronicle history to consider what a later playwright, John Ford, made of that genre in *Perkin Warbeck*. Instead of metamorphosing the English past into a type of Old Testament episode, as Heywood and Rowley had done, Ford uses the principle of analogy, rewriting earlier English history to make it resemble the contemporary situation in Germany. The hero of his play, Perkin Warbeck, a pretender to the English throne in the reign of Henry VII, recalls Charles I's brother-in-law, Frederick, the elector of the Palatinate and the pretender to the throne of Bohemia. England's failure to live up to its obligation, under both James and Charles, to come to Frederick's aid against his Catholic enemies and support the Protestant cause in Europe, is matched in the play by the Machiavellian reasoning of the king of Scotland, who also fails to live up to his promise to support Warbeck. Moreover, Warbeck's bride, the highly sympathetic Scottish princess Katherine, closely matches Elizabeth Stuart, Frederick's very popular wife, who was also the standard bearer of European Protestantism. The parallels are everywhere strongly implied, yet nowhere are they made explicit. Analogy and implication are sufficient to communicate the covert meaning of the play.

The readings of the plays presented in these chapters attempt to establish that playwrights could offer a variety of views on matters of religion, relying on the intelligence and subtlety of the cleverer members of their audience to apply or decode their message fully. Indeed so successful were these dramatists that no controversy apparently attended the performances of the plays discussed here. Those government agents who "geve allowance" evidently thought these works "meete to be plaied." As Stephen Greenblatt suggests, the master of the revels often regarded himself not as the strict censor of the theater but as its friendly guardian, charged with averting catastrophes. He was a bureaucrat concerned less with subversive ideas per se than with potential trouble. That is, there is no record of a dramatist being called to account for his heterodox beliefs; rather, plays were censored if they risked offending influential people, including important foreign allies, or if they threatened to cause public disorder by exacerbating religious or other controversies. The distinction is not a stable one, but it helps to explain the intellectual boldness, power, and freedom of a censored theater in a society in which the perceived enemies of the state were treated mercilessly.[21]

The works examined here clearly fit Greenblatt's description: they are hardly explicit in criticizing the dominant ideology, attacking individuals or allies, or proposing direct opposition to authorized policies. Such actions would have been dangerous. Only by using encoded or ambiguous presentations could playwrights raise doubts about government positions on religious questions and practices, expose inconsistencies, and suggest other points of view. How these playwrights succeeded in veiling their purposes and what these purposes were, are the subject of the following pages.

2

Dr. Faustus and the Religious Controversy

I

"CONTRITION, PRAYER, REPENTANCE: WHAT OF THEM?" Faustus asks, and the question Marlowe wrote for his hero echoed the uncertainty over religious beliefs and practices felt by many of Queen Elizabeth's subjects. As critics have long recognized, in *Doctor Faustus* Marlowe responded to this uncertainty by adapting the form of the English morality play. In this type of drama the soul of the hero, who stands for all humanity, is the focus of the struggle between the abstract forces of good and evil. According to Douglas Cole, "There is no doubt that the morality tradition provided Marlowe with both a thematic precedent and devices of dramaturgy on which to draw."[1]

The Good and Evil Angels who encourage Faustus, the Old Man who serves as a surrogate for the allegorical figure of Good Counsel, the pageant of the seven deadly sins—all are borrowed from the genre of the morality play, a type of entertainment that was performed well into the last quarter of the sixteenth century.[2] Yet Marlowe's reworking of this structure is hardly straightforward. Doctor Faustus cannot be considered an everyman figure, and Marlowe's hero is damned perpetually, quite unlike the usual conclusion to this form of drama which is "optimistic and constructive. [Morality plays tend to] . . . offer hope to the most desperate sinner with their constant message that while he is still alive it is never too late to repent."[3] Marlowe's work is not only more complex and sophisticated, more psychological and individualized, but may even be subversive. Nicolas Brooke, for example, has argued "that Marlowe's adoption of Morality form must be seen as a deliberate mis-use of popular old-fashioned material."[4] In support of this argument

22

Brooke points out that Faustus seems to be one who damns himself rather than, in the more traditional manner, becomes a victim of temptation; his fall is occasioned not by a failure of the will but rather by a resolute assertion of his ego. "Faustus is to be seen as choosing voluntarily, with knowledge of all that it means, Hell instead of Heaven. That is why I say that Marlowe has inverted the Morality structure: the course of Faustus's resolution is to damn himself; his temptation, his weakness, is in offers of repentance."[5] That Marlowe's hero is more active than passive is unquestionable; his blasphemy is shocking. And by his hero's behavior Marlowe has surely undermined the expectations of those familiar with the morality play tradition. But the degree to which Faustus can act with total freedom—in Brooke's words "choosing voluntarily"—is not quite so demonstrable as Brooke maintains. For matters of contrition, prayer, and repentance were themselves subjects of controversy in Marlowe's society.

Elizabeth's government was, in fact, expending much energy and determination in settling public uncertainties over just such beliefs and practices. For example, from 1576 to 1583 the queen, fearing that her vision of the Church of England would be undermined by his policies, even took the extreme step first of sequestering and then of permanently suspending Edmund Grindal, the man she had only recently named archbishop of Canterbury. Grindal believed that public preaching and discussion of the Bible would improve the clergy; Elizabeth realized that such gatherings or "prophesying," could be dominated by the disaffected and radical who would use these assemblies to undermine her church. Elizabeth's opinion was settled even if matters of religion were still hotly debated among her subjects.

The intense controversy and uncertainty that characterized matters of religious doctrine, practice, and belief are the true subjects of Marlowe's *Dr. Faustus*. Since these issues are a central concern of the play, we can only appreciate the work by understanding how greatly it reflects the contemporary climate. And we must consider as well the reasons why this play, among the most popular and frequently performed works of the entire period, never encountered difficulty with the censors, however liberal or incompetent they may have been.

In writing *Dr. Faustus*, Marlowe is sensitive to the growing debate among Protestants that became progressively more intense at his university during his years there. For unlike Oxford, Cambridge was the battlefield on which the Calvinist and Anti-Calvinist advocates played out their strategies, and the young Marlowe was surely an impressionable witness.[6] To appreciate the impact of this experience on him, we should know something of what he encountered as an undergraduate—the broad areas of disagreement that separated the various Protestant positions, the intense quarrels over religious doctrine, and the powerful impression created by influential churchmen. And we should also keep in mind that what may seem today to be minor differences took on importance because to a true believer such matters could prove decisive in the salvation of one's soul; the risks were very high.

Disagreements in matters of religion were, of course, nothing new to the English of the 1580s, for the populace was still feeling the effects of the Reformation—divided not only into Catholics and Protestants but also into varieties of Catholicism and Protestantism. Some Catholics considered themselves primarily English subjects and placed loyalty to the monarch above obedience to the Pope; others believed that true Catholicism could not be practiced without accepting the Pope's primacy of place. Among Protestants, too, the varieties of religious beliefs and practices as well as the intensity with which they were held defined the spectrum of English Protestantism in which the members of the Church of England could be more or less Calvinists.[7]

Quite naturally, many felt bewildered, estranged from their God. For some, the loss of the spiritual comfort afforded by the Catholic belief in purgatory, or in the effectiveness of prayers for the deceased, or in the practice of confession was made even more painful by the desecration of churches and by the elimination of ritual elements from the service. Moreover, the government understandably feared that religious radicalism would lead to political ferment and social unrest.[8] Those who claimed to be church reformers, some even preaching a new doctrine of egalitarianism, could make use of the tensions in society caused by economic problems (e.g. inflation) and social dislocations (e.g. land enclosure) to heighten the strains between rulers and ruled, between the wealthy and the impoverished. Elizabeth's administration happily adopted Archbishop Cranmer's forty-two Articles, now reduced to thirty-nine, since they were drafted in such a way that they could accommodate a variety of religious convictions. As Powell Mills Dawley has pointed out, the queen's "original settlement of religion had been constructed to rest on the broadest possible base of agreement on the essentials of Christian doctrine rather than on the precise and rigid theological definitions familiar in sixteenth-century confessional systems."[9] And so some matters were deliberately left unsaid or stated vaguely in an attempt to head off controversy. But in its effort to be all-encompassing, the Elizabethan settlement was rendered susceptible to influences from all directions, especially of those Reformed writings that issued from Geneva.

The initial efforts of the English Calvinists to correct what they saw as errors or abuses in the Church of England were focused on matters of polity and ritual. While they were prepared to accept episcopacy—on condition that the bishops were "godly"—the suspension of Grindal as archbishop led a significant number in the late 1570s to press for an alternate presbyterian system similar to that of Geneva, in which the clergy were elected by church members and matters of administration were shared by ministers and laymen. And they argued for the need to cleanse or purify the ceremonies of the church service from what they claimed were the remnants of popish customs— including such matters as the wearing of surplices and vestments, the location of the altar, and the practice of kneeling at prayer. According to Patrick Collinson, although these remained subjects of contention, the energy to sustain an active fight for such changes was waning by the end of the 1580s: the reformers were outmaneuvered, and the death of the earl of Leicester, one of their most influential supporters, proved a heavy loss.[10] In addition, the focus of attention during this period had been shifting from these operational concerns to doctrinal and philosophic matters that were closer to the heart of the differences between Calvinist and Anti-Calvinist views.[11] Nicholas Tyacke has neatly summarized how the balance of power changed in the next decade:

> In the early and middle years of Elizabeth's reign Calvinism keyed in fairly convincingly with political reality. To begin with, the existence of a large body of English Catholics lent credence to the identification of Protestants with the elect. Later, as relations with Spain

deteriorated, Calvinism was transferable to the international plane, and Englishmen were now portrayed as chosen by God to do battle for the true religion. But as political circumstances eased, so the way was open for undermining Calvinism from within. In the course of the 1590s the external threat from Spain appeared to diminish and the prospect of an internal revolt by English Catholics seemed increasingly remote. A united Protestant front was, therefore, less essential. At the same time English Calvinist teaching was itself becoming more extreme in line with continental religious developments.[12]

Now questions of grace and salvation came to the fore— questions that would be inescapable for the young Marlowe. Who were those elected to be saved? How could they know? How could salvation be assured? Could it be won or lost? Were some born reprobates, inevitably to be damned, and if so, when did God make this determination and why? These are indeed what were called "deep points."

> During the 1590s English Calvinism had been very much in the ascendant, and nowhere was that ascendancy more obvious than at Cambridge University. Symptomatic of the situation is the publication in 1590 of William Perkins's *Armilla Aurea* . . . [which] asserted the doctrine of absolute predestination against its critics . . . . Paradoxically, however, the propagation of such views also helped fuel the anti-Calvinist sentiment.[13]

The differences between English and Continental Protestantism were becoming increasingly difficult to ignore, and the hostility between those who held opposing points of view intensified. Through these quarrels, through public debate and preaching, ministers on both sides grew more outspoken, their skills sharper and more finely honed. As Patrick Collinson has remarked: Calvinist assumptions . . .

> were challenged, as they would not have been ten years before, by the reaction against Geneva which was gathering force amongst a party of avant-garde divines in Cambridge, and this nascent English 'Arminianism' would lend orthodox, Calvinist puritanism a new 'theological distinction.'[14]

Conditions were ripening for the forceful confrontations of the 1590s—the issues were more difficult and serious, the opponents more practiced and determined.

Enter Christopher Marlowe. On this scene of religious strife, Marlowe began his Cambridge University career as a student at Corpus Christi College in early December 1580. His program in his first year would have involved attending lectures in rhetoric (Quintilian, Hermogenes, and Cicero), preparing lessons for his tutor, studying the Old and New Testament, and attending chapel sermons.[15] Marlowe's arrival in Cambridge coincided with the period when William Perkins became known by his preaching as the most popular and effective spokesman for the extreme Calvinists. Perkins had received his B.A. in 1581 and his M.A. in 1584; in that year he was elected a fellow of Christ's, a position he was to hold for the next decade, and appointed lecturer at Great St. Andrews in the town. Perkins rapidly established himself both as a preacher and as "the most outstanding systematic Puritan theologian of his time."[16] Marlowe's career at Cambridge spans these years: he completed his undergraduate studies in 1584 when he was awarded his B.A.; and he continued in residence, with some periods of absence, until March 1587, when he filed his application for admission to the M.A. degree. His interest in the Faust story must have followed hard upon, for *The Tragical History of Dr. Faustus* was written sometime between 1588 and 1592—with many scholars giving it an earlier rather than later date.[17]

II

Since Perkins was among the most powerful voices at Cambridge during Marlowe's career there, we should consider what Calvinist principles he emphasized and how his presence may have influenced undergraduate attitudes. From firsthand accounts we know that he was an impressive and memorable teacher: according to Samuel Ward, who was trained at Christ's, "in expounding the commandments [Perkins] applied them so home, [that he was] able almost to make his hearers['] hearts fall down, and hairs to stand upright."[18] And in 1584 his appointment as lecturer at Great St. Andrews gave Perkins the opportunity to address an audience of both students and townspeople in Cambridge. His technique was clearly impressive. Even after the Civil War his fame was remembered.[19] Ultimately, two aspects of Perkins's manner account for his wide appeal—his arguments were constructed by a precise and logical method that applied the new Ramist principles of organization then in vogue, and his language was simple, direct, and moving. Perkins was so deeply persuaded of the importance of his mission and his words were chosen so carefully that a listener would find "his conscience so convinced, his secret faults so disclosed and his very heart so ripped up that he said, 'Certainly God speaks in this man.' "[20]

Naturally, Perkins's success aroused the Anti-Calvinist opposition and, feeling threatened, they began a counterattack. It is this controversy that provided the background for the debate Marlowe would dramatize in *Dr. Faustus*. But actually such tensions were nothing new among those holding differing views of what constituted the true doctrine of the Protestant church. Spokesmen for various points of view in the university had been sparring with one another throughout the 1580s, jockeying for lead position, attempting to attract converts, and vying for influence in the highest reaches of the English Church. An especially vivid instance of the intensity of the conflict between the two parties can be seen in the bitter quarrel that, after long smoldering, finally erupted in 1595–96 between William Barrett and Peter Baro, the Lady Margaret Professor of Divinity, on the one hand, and the heads and dons of the more Calvinist-oriented colleges on the other. Baro was accused of having "for the space of these fourteen or fifteen years, taught in his lectures, preached in sermons, determined in the Schools and printed in several books divers points of doctrine . . . contrary to that which hath been taught and received ever since her Majesty's reign, yet agreeable to the errors of Popery."[21]

Ironically, the views of Barrett and Baro were actually closer to the letter of the Thirty-nine Articles than were the theological positions of their opponents. Nevertheless, Perkins and his followers argued that their Calvinist opinions correctly expressed the spirit of the doctrines of the Church of England rightly understood, and that only those holding their views could think of themselves as true members of that Church. Their influence was so strong that Barrett was actually forced to recant and Baro was eased out of his position. Indeed, later church historians acknowledge the importance of Baro's role in curbing the growing power of the Calvinists: "this Doctrine finding many followers . . . might have quickly over-spread the whole University had it not been in part prevented and in part suppressed by the care and diligence of Dr. Barse [i.e. Baro] and his Adherents."[22]

III

Marlowe's *Dr. Faustus* directly engages these controversies.[23] His plot roughly follows the story-line of the English *Faustbook*, but the issues it raises are not discussed in this source. The theological significance of Dr. Faustus's choices can perhaps best be understood by referring to what Perkins himself wrote in a work that, as Ian Breward notes, "grew out of sermons in the 1590's, when a fresh outbreak of popular interest in the discovery and detection of witches would make it a very topical treatment."[24] According to Perkins, the practice of witchcraft is like the sin in Eden of desiring to become a god, motivated by a longing either to win "credit and countenance amongst men" or, "not satisfied with the measure of inward gifts received, as of knowledge, wit, understanding, memory and suchlike, . . . to search out such things as God would have kept secret."[25] This is what Marlowe describes as the "world of profit and delight, / Of power, of honor, of omnipotence:" his hero wants "to practise more than heavenly power permits." Now "having commencde"—or taken his degree[26]—Faustus would exceed "Emperours and Kings," for they

> Are but obeyd in their severall provinces:
> . . . .
> But his dominion that exceedes in this,
> Stretcheth as farre as doth the mind of man.
> A sound Magician is a mighty god:
> Heere Faustus trie thy braines to gaine a deitie.[27]
> (I.i.88–93)

To describe him in Perkins's words, Marlowe's Faustus is "not satisfied" with the achievements of his education. Had he been a student at Cambridge, for example, his program of study—disputations in divinity (e.g. on such topics as free will, justification, and grace), systematic and analytic sermons on Biblical passages, and the presentation and defense of theses—would have trained him in such matters as God would not have kept secret from us. To conduct these disputations, analyses, and defenses, the study of logic or dialectics was prescribed in the undergraduate curriculum in the third and fourth years. Aristotle was the required text; as Faustus says, he would "live and die in Aristotles workes." But in his next thought, "*Bene disserere est finis logicis.* / Is, to dispute well, Logickes chiefest end," Faustus quotes and translates a precept of the controversial French reformer, Peter Ramus, who advocated revising the traditional scholasticism of the university curriculum that blended Aristotle with St. Thomas Aquinas.

By their efforts, the Ramists attempted to simplify and clarify the methods of the scholastics and to systematize the reasoning processes—especially on the correct way to establish truth through logic. Perkins, for one, retained the scholastic method for discussing questions of divinity, but he was a Ramist in his arguments. For analyzing matters of church doctrine his preferred method was an orderly, step-by-step sequence of questions and answers. As described by Peter Helyn, who was perhaps rephrasing Thomas Fuller's words, "when he was a Catechist of Christs Colledge in Cambridge [Perkins] did lay the Law so home in the ears of his Auditors that it made their hearts fall down, and yea their hair to stand almost upright."[28] Catechisms were a common element in teaching the principles of the reformed churches: "a huge number appeared in England between 1558 and 1660, frequently written by those with puritan sympathies, aimed not only at supplementing or replacing the brief catechism in the Prayer Book, but also seeking to provide godly householders with material with which to edify their family and servants."[29] Perkins offers a fine example in his *The Foundation of Christian Religion Gathered into Six Principles* (1590), in which he carefully makes the fine distinctions that will help one think correctly on religious matters:

> Question: What state shall the wicked be in after the day of judgment?

Answer: In eternal perdition and destruction in hell-fire.
Question: What is that?
Answer: It stands in three things especially: first, a perpetual sepa-
          ration from God's presence; secondly, fellowship with the
          devil and his angels; thirdly, an horrible pang and torment
          both of body and soul arising of the feeling of the whole
          wrath of God, poured forth on the wicked for ever, world
          without end; and if the pain of one tooth for one day be so
          great, endless shall be the pain of the whole man, body
          and soul for ever.[30]

Faustus makes use of just this kind of catechism when he first
talks with Mephostophilis. For the most part, his lines are a series of questions to which Mephostophilis provides the answers:
"Tell me what is that Lucifer thy Lord?" "Was not that Lucifer
an Angell once?" "How comes it then that he is prince of di-
vels?" "And what are you that live with Lucifer?" "Where are
you damn'd?" "How comes it then that thou art out of hel?"
(I.iii.288–300).

Despite all of his advanced studies and perceptive questions,
Faustus is completely unaware of his ignorance and blinded by
his self-conceit.[31] In his opening soliloquy in which he debates the
merits of various fields of endeavor, Faustus rejects Aristotelian
logic as a subject worthy of his attention and considers medicine
as a possible career. But once again, his aspirations are blasphemous. Faustus could be satisfied as a physician only if he had
the godlike power to grant immortality—to "make man to live
eternally / Or being dead, raise them to life againe." Medicine, it
appears, is too restrictive for one with his ambitions. And, after
thinking about it, he determines his disposition is also unsuited
for the law, for Faustus has neither the patience nor the interpre-
tive skills to interest himself in what he calls "paltry legacies."
Faustus even admits that he cannot distinguish "a petty case"
from much more important instances—for example, under what
circumstances a father may disinherit a son: "Ex haereditari fil-
ium non potest pater nisi." This topic is, in fact, one discussed
not only by Justinian but also by Protestant clerics: in spiritual
terms, when and under what conditions does God decide to dis-
own his child? Faustus is like the man described by Perkins in a
sermon delivered in 1593:

a sinner in his first estate . . . hath a veil before his face so that he seeth nothing. The wrath of God and the curse due for sin, hell and damnation seeking to devour him he seeth them not . . . but rusheth securely into all manner of sin, the night of impenitence and the mist of ignorance so blinding his eyes that he seeth not the narrow bridge of this life, from which if he slide he falls immediately into the bottomless pit of hell.[32]

Unable to reason properly and, as Perkins describes it, "not resting content with the condition of men," hoping to be "a mighty god," to be "on earth as Jove is in the skie," Faustus rejects Jerome's Bible for "Negromantike bookes."

In the play each of these subjects has its advocate, the Good Angel naturally promoting the joys of Bible study and the Evil Angel recommending the advantages of black magic. Whether they are reflections of Faustus's own mental processes or independent of them, these allegorical figures objectify the inner conflict in the hero; through them the contest for his soul is dramatized. And what at first seems most important is that they emphasize his freedom to choose. If Faustus were born to be damned, as he might be in a Calvinistic universe, he is surely ignorant of it, for he believes he can exercise his own will. Yet he admits that the rewards promised by the Evil Angel are irresistible. Since Faustus is actually the type of person who is drawn compulsively to what is blasphemous, daring, and imprudent, it is not at all clear that his choice is so free after all. The A-text, in lines that do not appear in the 1616 edition, emphasizes how greatly his decision is a consequence of his character:

> not your words onely, but mine owne fantasie,
> That will receive no object for my head,
> But ruminates on Negromantique skill.
> (I.i.136–38)[33]

The force of his own nature compels him to the study of magic, and he is unable to resist: "Tis Magicke, Magicke that hath ravisht mee."[34] Faustus signs his pact with the devil, providing, as Perkins explains, "the ground of all the practices of witchcraft: . . . a league or covenant made between the witch and the devil wherein they do mutually bind themselves to each other."[35]

Faustus reminds himself repeatedly of the price he will ultimately pay if he continues, and he realizes, at least in a part of his mind, that reformation and repentance are more than "vaine fancies." But Faustus lacks faith, and that is essential for salvation. Acknowledging that in his case "the god thou servest is thine owne appetite," he rightly concludes that he "must . . . needes be damnd." His inability to give up the pursuit of magic or break his agreement with Lucifer, then, can explain, according to Anti-Calvinist teaching, why he is ultimately damned or, according to Calvinist teaching, why he was born damned. As Perkins reminds his congregation, "the decree of God in rejecting some is unsearchable."[36]

The ending of the play merits especially close attention, for it focuses explicitly on the conflicting Calvinist and Anti-Calvinist views. According to the Old Man, Faustus can still be saved: he has only to "call for mercie and avoyd dispaire." Just such a line of reasoning would be held by Perkins's opponent, Peter Baro, who argued that "to each and every man God desires to give grace sufficient for salvation, for Christ died for each and every man."[37] Though some may choose to resist it—"the grace which is offered they thrust from them" in Hooker's words—saving grace is available to all.[38] The Old Man's encouragement to Faustus would certainly support such a reading: "I see an Angell hovers ore thy head, / And with a violl full of precious grace, / Offers to powre the same into thy soule." It is only by rejecting the grace that is freely offered that one becomes a reprobate: as Baro explained, "Men shut themselves out of heaven, not God."[39] In its ending the text of the play can be made to support the non-Calvinist view that Faustus can still attain salvation by an act of faith, by repentance and prayer. The obstacle is not God's witholding of grace, but Faustus's belief that he is unable to seize it. His faith proves too weak and insufficient: "I do repent, and yet I do dispaire." He cannot believe he can be forgiven by the God he "hath abjurde . . . whome Faustus hath blasphemed."[40] According to the Old Man, Faustus is "accursed" because he "excludst the grace of heaven." But Faustus has always thought of himself as beyond common humanity. Since to his mind superlative and excessive actions are the hallmarks of his nature, his offenses must naturally be so great that he "can nere be pardoned, / The Serpent that tempted Eve may be sav'd / But not Faustus." As Wilbur Sanders has observed, "We are watching a man . . . locked in a death embrace with the agonising God he can neither reject nor love. It is the final consummation of the Puritan imagination."[41] Much as he may desire it, Faustus's conception of himself prevents him from achieving justifying faith.[42]

The Anti-Calvinist, emphasizing the hero's need to turn to God and believe in his forgiveness, can, of course, be countered by stressing those elements that make Faustus seem more a Calvinist paradigm. Read in that light he is quite simply one born a reprobate who will feel God's "heavy wrath."[43] He was damned from birth: "You starres that raignd at my nativitie, / whose influence hath alotted death and hel."[44] In the final judgment his fate was not determined by Faustus' deeds or lack of faith. According to Perkins, the decision who shall be saved and who condemned is God's alone; it "hath not any cause beside his will and pleasure."[45] The saving drop of Christ's blood is denied him as it is to all reprobates who, in the words of Perkins:

> are punished with eternal confusion and most bitter reproaches. . . . They have fellowship with the devil and his angels. They are wholly in body and soul tormented with an incredible horror and exceeding great anguish, through the sense and feeling of God's wrath poured out upon them forever.[46]

Marlowe's work directs the attention of Elizabethan laymen to the variety of beliefs held on such religious issues as predestination. Many of Marlowe's countrymen in Canterbury refused to take much of what their Calvinist-oriented preachers said to heart, maintaining a faith that was simpler and more direct. He may well have known that some men of his father's generation, in the part of England where he was raised, found the doctrine of predestination particularly offensive:

> Reports reached the Privy Council in 1550 of a group of Kentish men from around Maidstone and Faversham who had been affirming that "the doctrine of predestination was meter for devils than for christian men." Their leader, Henry Harte, had taught publicly "that there is no man so chosen or predestinate, but that he may condemn himself; neither is there any so reprobate but that he may, if he will, keep the commandments and be saved."

He had also boasted that "his faith was not grounded upon learned men, for all errors were brought in by learned men." Humphrey Middleton, one of Harte's followers, phrased the concept of universal salvation in a different way: "since Adam was elected to salvation, and since all men, being then in Adam's loins, were also predestined to salvation, therefore there could be none predestined to reprobation."[47]

Such members of the audience watching *Dr. Faustus* who were followers of Harte would have argued that the play's hero is damned simply because he condemns himself: he will not "keep the commandments and be saved." And, at least in Kent, such practical common sense remained widespread even into the early years of James's reign. In 1604, Josias Nicholls, a Kentish minister, spoke of

> a parish of four hundred communicants where a policy of systematic catechizing before administering the sacraments had revealed that scarcely one in ten was familiar with the elements of protestant doctrine. Asked "whether it were possible for a man to live so uprightlie that by well doing he might winne heaven," there was hardly a man who failed to answer in the affirmative: "that a man might be saved by his owne weldoing, and that he trusted he did so live that by God's grace hee shoulde obtaine everlasting life, by serving God and good prayers, etc."[48]

But perhaps the best summary statement of this attitude was made by George Gifford, the Puritan vicar and preacher of Malden, who has been called a "Tudor anthropologist" for his subtle and sharp-eyed comments on behavior.[49] According to Gifford, the beliefs found among "the common sort of christians" are simple and straightforward: "I meane well; I hurte no man: nor I thinke no man anye hurt; I love God above all; and put my whole trust in him. What woulde you have more? They preache and teache, [but] they can tell us no more but this when they have said all what they can."[50] This offers a very practical and direct way of analyzing the action of Marlowe's play. In the eyes of such an audience, the work might have been thought controversial or "subversive," for it presents a very harsh and unforgiving deity. Yet the play itself could hardly be regarded as radical; the play's author or actors could not have been in danger of arrest by local authorities for failing to uphold the orthodox teachings of church and state. But the ways that such a play can affect an audience are complex and insidious.

As a consequence, such plays as Marlowe's would have forced audiences to question their response to that which received official authorization and endorsement, to consider where they positioned themselves within ideology.[51]

IV

Can one fix the ultimate responsibility, however? Is Faustus a Calvinist reprobate, a being born to be damned, one so fixed in his ways that from birth the course of his life is a foregone conclusion? Alan Sinfield has succinctly expressed this point of view: "Marlowe's Faustus is not damned because he is wicked, but wicked because he is damned."[52] Or on the contrary, is Faustus an Arminian soul, a free agent exercising volition who refuses the grace that is freely given? In the words of Roma Gill, "Marlowe's God is more long-suffering than the God of the Elizabethan church and continues to extend mercy and forgiveness to Faustus long after the traditional God would have turned away."[53] Clearly, in either case, the spiritual failure in the hero's character is a crucial element in the outcome, but in the final analysis, the issue remains unresolved and unresolvable. Both Calvinist and Anti-Calvinist views are sustained throughout the action. For this reason, as Alan Sinfield has observed in a recent study, the play is ultimately disturbing:

> Faustus is amenable at every point, I think, to a determined orthodox reading. Yet the play might do more to promote anxiety about such doctrine than to reinforce it. For although I have felt it necessary to argue for a Reformation reading, Faustus is in my view entirely ambiguous—altogether open to the more usual, modern, free-will reading. The theological implications of Faustus are radically and provocatively indeterminate.[54]

And this indeterminacy, this deliberate ambivalence, presumably enabled the play to escape the censor.

In no small measure Marlowe's experiences at Cambridge helped shape his hero who is neither clearly redeemable nor reprobate: ultimately, the play cannot be reduced to a straightforward theological text.[55] The reasons for what Norman Rabkin would call its "complementarity," however, are surely personal and practical as well as religious.[56] We need not read *Dr. Faustus* as reflecting quite so extreme a psychological crisis as Wilbur Sanders does, who holds responsible "those disordered forces in Marlowe's own imagination which lead him either into hectic exaggeration or into moralistic excess."[57] Yet we should acknowledge that the young playwright was not only reacting to the fierce debate between Calvinists and Anti-Calvinists he had witnessed as a Cambridge undergraduate but also incorporating into the poetry something of his own personal reaction to this debate. While a divinity student he had, after all, heard some of the most forceful and unforgettable presentations of the extreme Calvinist position: even as an old man, Peter Helyn could still recall that William Perkins would "pronounce the word *Damne* with so strong an Emphasis that it left an echo in the ears of his hearers a long time after."[58]

When designing his play in the late 1580s or early 1590s, Marlowe must have also taken into account political and aesthetic considerations. He was surely aware of the long-standing government prohibition against those who "handle in their plaies certen matters of Divinytie and of State unfitt to be suffred." Indeed, perhaps as a consequence of the Martin-Marprelate imbroglio, the authorities were once again feeling the need for more forceful control over the stage: in November 1589 the Privy Council requested that Archbishop Whitgift appoint a "fytt persone well learned in Divinity" to assist the master of the revels in screening plays "to geve allowance of suche as they shall thincke meete to be plaied and to forbydd the rest."[59] The performance history of Marlowe's effort clearly indicates that it did not defy the censors, however much it might have ruffled the feathers of one or another religious flock. And whether the result of his practical good sense, of his instincts as an artist, or of some combination of the two, Marlowe must have understood that a work that engages in so hotly contested a subject would surely attract the public, just as he must have realized that any play with a clear-cut or consistent theological message could easily turn into something didactic, undramatic, or dangerous.

The energy of his work, its power to draw an audience, would be generated by playing off the possibility of salvation against the fear of absolute damnation, an Anti-Calvinist worldview, expressed through the Good Angel, in conflict with a Calvinist hero, a born reprobate. And this combination would enable him to create a memorable character. After all, a protagonist presented purely in a Calvinist light, one who can do nothing to assure his own salvation, is merely a victim—rather like the pathetic figure of the *de casibus* tradition. And the other alternative, a protagonist who is completely responsible for his damnation, is liable to appear merely wicked or foolish—rather like the title character in a Senecan-styled tragedy. A hero of either stamp could arouse little interest.

In the final analysis, then, Marlowe's drama can be appreciated as the product of a number of forces—the controversy between Calvinists and Anti-Calvinists that must have impressed him deeply during his years at Cambridge, the expanding power of state censorship which could be rigorously enforced, and, surely not to be underestimated, his own personal, poetic, and artistic instincts.

3

Measure for Measure: Saints' Lives and "Heavenly Comforts"

LIKE MARLOWE'S *DR. FAUSTUS*, SHAKESPEARE'S *MEASURE FOR Measure* treats religious issues in profoundly troubling ways. But unlike Marlowe, who looks at two different branches of Protestantism, Shakespeare focuses on issues distinctive of both Protestantism and Catholicism. Although such a play in other hands might have served to offer confirmation and reassurance of either Catholic or Protestant belief, *Measure for Measure* opens both religions to uneasy doubts; ultimately, what might have been a dramatization reaffirming a particular religion's doctrine ends by making religious teachings appear questionable, objectionable, or even incomprehensible.

And indeed, the treatment of Papists and Puritans was a subject of some special interest during the summer of 1604 when Shakespeare was working on his play, for *Measure for Measure* seems to have been first acted then and presented at court on 26 December 1604. This was a crucial period in the new king's reign. Having now been on the throne for more than a year, James was asserting himself with greater forcefulness in matters of religion. In February 1604, John Chamberlain noted that the Crown was taking more vigorous action against Catholics: the fines imposed on them during the reign of Elizabeth were being reinstituted. James had ordered a temporary respite in these taxes, since "not any one of them had lift[ed] up his Hand against his coming in, and so he gave them a Year of Probation to conform themselves, which seeing it had not wrought that Effect, he had fortified all the Laws that were against them, and made them stronger." So James, who was hardly partial to the Puritans, was now balancing the severity of his rule in the treatment of all Nonconformists. As Chamberlain concludes, "Our Puritans go down on all sides. . . . But now to make all even . . . the Papists should not take heart upon the depressing of the Puritans . . . with a vaine Hope of Tolleration."[1] Yet the Papists could not be without any hope, for James signed the Treaty of London in August 1604, bringing an end to the war with Spain, abandoning his Dutch Protestant allies, and making many of his new subjects intensely uneasy.

The beliefs of both Papists and Puritans are reflected in the characters in Shakespeare's play. But the work, evenhanded in its consideration of Catholic and Protestant precepts, presents a skeptical point of view and evades the possible objections of the Revels Office by its deliberate indeterminacy.[2] Indeed, it dramatizes this skepticism with deftness and subtlety—or to use the words of Richard Dutton, "provocative opinion . . . suitably veiled."[3]

As a shaping form for his drama Shakespeare, like Marlowe, seems to have looked back to the didactic and moralistic entertainments of the recent past. And just as Marlowe adapted and even radicalized the form of the morality play for his own purposes, Shakespeare reformulates elements of an earlier genre to disturb his audience. This procedure has decided advantages. From their previous experiences in the theater both playwright and playgoer could anticipate that conventional situations and characters would meet with conventional, predictable responses. But in Shakespeare's treatment of the conventional, expectation is unfulfilled and what could have been conventional has been reformulated in surprising ways. For example, the plotting of *Measure for Measure* involves subjects we might expect to find in a saint's life play, yet ultimately this work denies the principles and fails to arouse the emotional responses traditionally associated with this genre.

Indeed, we may come to a new appreciation of the richness and complexity of Shakespeare's achievement by considering his work in the context of the medieval saint's life play or even that sourcebook for such plays, the thirteenth century compendium of saints' lives, Jacobus de Voragine's *The Golden Legend*. Even though few examples have survived into the twentieth century— aside from the Cornish *St. Meriasek*, only two late fifteenth century texts are extant—what little we know in general about this genre can account for much that we continue to find troubling and confusing in *Measure for Measure*.[4] By simply isolating basic threads of the story line of Shakespeare's drama, we can actually make a rather straightforward case for linking Shakespeare's work with this medieval material. For example, a play in which the protagonist is a novice in a religious order, is described as "a thing enskied and sainted," and has her faith and values severely tested by the incidents of the plot surely suggests the story of a saint's life. Moreover, in none of the generally acknowledged sources for *Measure for Measure* is the prototype for Shakespeare's Isabella particularly religious; so far as we know of earlier treatments of similar material, Shakespeare's heroine differs from her precursors in her desire for holiness as well as in her asceticism and spiritual dedication.

Tracing specific ways in which the medieval saint's life plays may have influenced a much later drama is especially worth undertaking since it may help us understand what presuppositions and preconceptions the Elizabethans brought to their theater. It is only by understanding the usual practices, the accepted, ongoing conventions that we can begin to appreciate how the religious and literary landscape appeared to them. After all, the tradition of dramatizing the lives of saints for religious or political purposes was widespread and deeply rooted in England. The popularity, variety, and longevity of such plays suggest that their impact on the drama that followed must have been considerable: from extant town, church, and guild records we know that at least thirty-eight different saints had at least sixty-six different plays written about them.[5] These works were performed from the mid-thirteenth century to the first half of the sixteenth century: a play on St. Nicholas was mentioned c. 1250, and the last known English saint play, on Thomas the Apostle, was performed at York in 1535.[6] After the Reformation, John Bale and other Protestant polemicists turned the lives of the saints into plays that suited the new politics and the new religion.[7] As a consequence an Elizabethan audience would not have been surprised, presumably, by characters, behavior, or events that may trouble a modern audience. As Catherine Belsey has observed, "the prevalence of particular theatrical conventions in given periods implies that the previous experience of the audience in the theater itself has an influence on their expectations, their beliefs about what is plausible, and their willingness to accept certain relationships and connections without detailed exposition by the dramatist each time they recur."[8] And while the audience would quickly recognize the pattern of a saint's life tradition, it would also be sensitive to subtle variations, or traces of irony, or unusual treatments in Shakespeare's use of this material.

For a number of reasons *Measure for Measure* would remind an Elizabethan theatergoer of a saint's life play. First of all, its plot involves the subjects one might expect to find in such works. As John Wasson has pointed out, such plays invariably dramatized a limited number of stories: the martydrom of a saint, the conversion of a sinner, or the force of divine intervention into earthly affairs.[9] In *Measure for Measure*, Shakespeare manages to combine all of these. In its action Shakespeare's comedy can be regarded as a "martyrdom" play, dramatizing the strength and determination of Isabella, the novice, to hold on to her beliefs. It can also be considered a "conversion" play, showing how the sinner Angelo undergoes reformation through the teaching of the Duke, Isabella, and Mariana. And it can be seen as a work that illustrates the power of a saint or Providence to perform miraculous deeds—the Duke, "like Power divine," makes everything come out right, or nearly right, in the end.

In its individual details Shakespeare's drama also recalls elements that are commonly found in the stories of the lives of saints. Like these, his is filled with torment and tortures as well as miracles and repentances, the very stuff of such works. Much of the action takes place in a gloomy prison. The horror of the place and its grim reality are reinforced not only by references to hanging and beheading, practices supervised by the executioner Abhorson, but also by the sight of the severed head of the pirate Ragozine, which is actually carried on stage in Act IV. In short, the action can be described as dramatizing the absolute purity of the holy saint, the cruelty of her tormentor, and the fearfulness of the pain and death that the tormentor can command.

As a "martyrdom" play, the action focuses on Isabella who is first seen preparing to enter the order of St. Clare. Although noted for their austerity, the practices of these nuns are more liberal than Isabella expects, for she was "rather wishing a more strict restraint / Upon the sisters" than those described by her instructress:

> When you have vow'd, you must not speak with men
> But in the presence of the prioress;
> Then, if you speak, you must not show your face;
> Or if you show your face, you must not speak.
>
> (I.iv.10–13)[10]

Isabella's devotion has clearly turned her into a rigid, absolute, and cold creature. Indeed, much about her suggests comparison with the most severe and devoted of the popular saints and martyrs described in *The Golden Legend.* Like St. Katherine, who "confounded" fifty learned philosophers and "surmounted all mortal men in worldly wisdom," Isabella "hath prosperous art / When she will play with reason and discourse, / And well she can persuade." (I.ii.174–76)[11] And like this saint, Isabella is undaunted by threats and cruelty; she might well repeat St. Katherine's words, "Whatever torments thou canst devise . . . delay them not, for I desire to offer my flesh and blood to Christ." She regards the proposition of Angelo, "the new deputy now for the duke," as a testing of her faith. To save her brother she is told:

> Lay by all nicety and prolixious blushes
> That banish what they sue for. Redeem thy brother
> By yielding up thy body to my will;
> Or else he must not only die the death,
> But thy unkindness shall his death draw out
> To ling'ring sufferance.
>
> (II.iv.161–66)

With the absolute determination of a martyr, transforming physical pain into spiritual pleasure, Isabella rejects the advances of the sadistic Angelo:

> were I under the terms of death,
> Th'impression of keen whips I'd wear as rubies,
> And strip myself to death as to a bed
> That longing have been sick for, ere I'd yield
> My body up to shame.
>
> (II.iv.99–104)

When the setting moves into the prison, we witness the terror facing Isabella's brother, Claudio, and hear his impassioned plea to her to save his life. "Death is a fearful thing," he cries, and implores, "Sweet sister, let me live." Their confrontation enables Isabella to make clear the depth of her commitment to her calling:

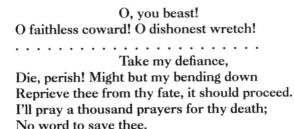

> O, you beast!
> O faithless coward! O dishonest wretch!
> . . . .
>   Take my defiance,
> Die, perish! Might but my bending down
> Reprieve thee from thy fate, it should proceed.
> I'll pray a thousand prayers for thy death;
> No word to save thee.
>   (III.i.135–46)

Puzzling in its unchristian lack of compassion and even repellent to a modern audience, her harsh rejection can be seen as a demonstration of her belief that a saintly character is unwavering in her vows of chastity. Following the conventional behavior pattern of saints in *The Golden Legend*—and presumably of their lives as they were enacted on the medieval stage—Isabella remains unshaken in her faith and absolute in her purity, rather reminding one of a St. Margaret, who, having just converted them, watched with equanimity as five thousand of her followers were beheaded.[12] Isabella's absolute intransigence, holding fast to the narrow conditions of her faith—which allows her to express little sympathy for her brother—proves how profound are both her spiritual convictions and her determination to follow the dictates of her religion.

But Shakespeare's work is not simply an elaboration of the "martyrdom" type of saint's life play. By shifting our attention from Isabella to Angelo, we can regard the action as dramatizing the nearly miraculous and sudden transformation of a cruel oppressor into a repentant sinner—like the conversion of the cruel and wicked king in the legend of St. Christopher.[13] Indeed, *Measure for Measure* examines the stages of the deputy's development. His sexual attraction to Isabella, intensified by the fact that her inhibitions are identical to his own, unleashes the lascivious side of his nature. And so someone who took pride in the fact that he was highly regarded as "a man of stricture and firm abstinence," who "scarce confesses / That his blood flows; or that his appetite / Is more to bread than stone," (I.iii.53–54), suddenly finds himself lacking in self-control: "now I give my sensual race the rein" (II.iv.159). The action of the play then traces the ways in which Angelo is brought to confession, penance, and reformation. First, he expresses his own sense of shame and regret: "Alack, when once our grace we have forgot, / nothing goes right; we would, and we would not" (IV.iv.31–32). And ultimately through the forgiveness of Isabella, the love of Mariana, and the ministrations of the Duke, the deputy can find his way to absolution. Despite the extreme evil of his character and his persistence in denying his guilt, Angelo, like the repentant tyrant in *The Golden Legend*, suddenly manifests the capacity for change:

> O my dread lord,
> I should be guiltier than my guiltiness
> To think I can be undiscernible,
> When I perceive your Grace, like power divine,
> Hath looked upon my passes.
>
> (V.i.364–368)

His reformation becomes more comprehensible if we recognize that the traces of a second kind of saint's life play, the reformation of the lost soul, are also being dramatized in his story.

The third category of saint's life play, proving that God works in mysterious ways or that saints and Providence can perform miraculous deeds, is demonstrated in the sometimes peculiar actions of Duke Vincentio. Indeed, it is his behavior that is often most puzzling to a modern audience. But the Duke is, after all, a character whose abilities approach the superhuman. He is the controlling force of the action—appointing Angelo as his surrogate, overhearing Claudio's interview with Isabella, introducing Isabella to Mariana, encouraging Mariana to act as her replacement, and, finally, choreographing the sequence of revelations at the conclusion. Though neither omnipresent nor omnipotent, the

Duke clearly has mastered the art of being in just the right place at just the right time and with just the right information. Duke Vincentio forgives the sinner—he even absolves the unrepentant Barnardine: "for those earthly faults, I quit them all." He stage-manages the discovery of Claudio's escape from death with a maximum of wonder and surprise. And significantly taking on a godlike stance, he is the only character in the play who addresses the audience directly, delivering a homily on the responsibility of rulers.

Moreover, for most of the action Shakespeare's Duke is in disguise while he arranges for the happy ending. In all these respects he is much like one of those saints who manages to perform many of his good works while trying to conceal his true identity.[14] And like the earlier miracle play, which demonstrates the basic Christian principle that Providence can use extraordinary means to comfort us, *Measure for Measure* considers charity, forgiveness, and love as sources for true happiness.

Yet to see *Measure for Measure* simply as a combination of elements derived from the saint's life play cannot account for everything we find in it.[15] Even if theatrical conventions tend to condition audience expectations, spectators at *Measure for Measure* could hardly anticipate the unusual way the action would reach its resolution. Indeed, Jean Howard finds that Shakespeare's play even challenges the emotional and intellectual range of the comic genre itself, taking "a series of radically unexpected turns which, to a greater extent than is true in the nonproblem comedies, destabilize audience expectations and call in question, not just the strength of the play's final resolution, but the adequacy of comic conventions to contain the intractible and complicated matter of the play's vision."[16] For example, although Isabella's intransigence may bring to mind something of the saintly behavior found in heroines of an earlier type of medieval drama, her lack of charity for her brother—she calls him a "beast," a "faithless coward," a "dishonest wretch"—is hard to reconcile with traditional notions of mercy and forgiveness, virtues Isabella comes to praise at the end of the play. And ultimately, the novice, once convinced that she was destined to become one of the sisters of St. Clare, discovers that her true vocation may not be found in a cloister after all. Indeed, rather than being fixed like St. Margaret in a state of absolute spiritual assurance, Isabella seems to undergo a remarkable change when she joins Mariana in pleading for Angelo's life. Her new understanding, her change in attitude, suggests how much more complex the basic story material has become when it is transformed into post-Reformation drama. And as if to point up her dilemma as a character, Shakespeare leaves her status unresolved, for she never responds to the unexpected marriage proposal of the Duke.[17]

Angelo's nature, too, is problematic. Although he may be cast in the role of the reformed tyrant of the saint's life play, he is too psychologized to enact this part as a simple, converted villain of medieval religious drama. In Shakespeare's hands, he becomes a man who quite deliberately attempts to sustain to the very last moment the fraud he has constructed to hide the truth of his behavior. Since he admits to this truth only when he knows he can no longer persist in lying, Angelo is a somewhat unsatisfying character—one might have expected a lengthier, more introspective statement of his remorse. Indeed, when finally confronted with the evidence of his guilt, he expresses not so much a Christian conversion to a new life as a desperate plea for death in what sounds like a belief in a predestined, Calvinist end:

> Then, good prince,
> No longer session hold upon my shame,
> But let my trial be mine own confession,
> Immediate sentence, then, and sequent death
> Is all the grace I beg.
>
> (V.i.368–371)

And even after he has married an all-forgiving Mariana and heard Isabella's elaborately reasoned plea for his life, Angelo repeats his request for execution:

> I am sorry and such sorrow I procure,
> And so deep sticks it in my penitent heart
> That I crave death more willingly than mercy;
> 'Tis my deserving, and I do entreat it.
>
> (V.i.472–475)

How are we to understand the moral state of one who twice insists that he prefers death to mercy?

Finally, Vincentio, the duke of Vienna, is also troubling, for as an authority figure he has only questionable ability. He nearly fails to save Claudio from execution; he cannot bring Barnardine to repent; and to his own surprise, he finds himself emotionally attracted to Isabella—after deliberately causing her some rather puzzling moments of intense anguish. He seems an odd, almost slipshod miracle worker who very nearly fails to come to the rescue of a hard-pressed humanity. In his instance, the active involvement of saints in human affairs is a questionable matter. The age of miracles has passed, and the deity is remote: *deus absconditus*.

Ultimately, then, to explain these difficulties one might well argue that Shakespeare is recalling earlier saint's life stories; but, far from merely imitating them, he uses them for ironic or disturbing purposes, dramatizing how essentially Catholic paradigms of holiness, redemption, and salvation were called into question by the Reformation, emptied of their religious aura. Shakespeare's public was much less uniform in its religious beliefs than the audience of his predecessors. The world of *Measure for Measure* is in need of spiritual salvation, but the unquestioning presentation of religious matters typical of medieval Catholic drama has here given way to a problematic treatment. Its indeterminacy—the troubling variations from medieval orthodoxy that color Shakespeare's handling of plot and character in this work—may reflect the continuing uncertainties of their religious convictions experienced by both Catholics and Protestants in a new, post-Reformation age.[18]

II

These spiritual uncertainties are also addressed through the play's almost obsessive involvement with death. In our discussion of the work as a saint's life play, for instance, we touched upon its pervasive concern with the necessity of confronting the fact of one's own death (for example, Claudio) or of the death of a loved one (Isabella, Mariana). Through its concentration on this subject Shakespeare's play raises additional questions about the religious convictions of its audience. Although the confrontation with death can quickly lead one to despair, it is a distinctively Protestant notion that being reduced to a state of despair can result in "heavenly comforts." To those of a logical turn of mind, the reasoning sounds at best paradoxical if not contradictory—like the imprisoned Claudio, sentenced to die, we might well ask "What's the comfort?" Yet this painful spiritual condition is highly desirable, according to the ruler of Vienna, who combines by position and disguise both political power and religious authority. And his view is not idiosyncratic: the benefits of despair are not to be underestimated, for the belief that the loss of hope in salvation is a prerequisite to salvation finds confirmation in the Church of England and in the sermons of influential members of the English Protestant clergy in the late sixteenth century.

In Renaissance thinking, despair can produce two contradictory spiritual states. On the one hand, as in traditional Catholic doctrine, to doubt God's power to grant remission for one's sins is to demonstrate a lack of faith that will result in damnation. But on the other hand, according to the argument developed by Luther and Calvin, despair marks the very start of one's spiritual recovery.[19] Both of these reformers, in fact, found "a kind of self-despair as prerequisite to salvation," and, no doubt under their influence, Protestant sermons on the Continent stressed the need for fallen humanity, aware of its unworthiness, to be reborn by completely depending on God. "For except thou have born the cross of adversity and temptation, and hast felt thyself brought unto the very brim of desperation, yea, and unto hell-gates . . . it shall not be possible for thee to think that God is righteous and just."[20] It was this line of reasoning that found adherents not only in Protestant churches in Germany and Switzerland but also in those that followed the more liberal brand of Protestantism established by the Anglican Church. Despair, as Robert Burton explained in *The Anatomy of Melancholy*, could affect even "God's best children."[21] As a result, the spiritual struggle of working through a deeply troubled conscience to arrive at a renewed, positive reliance on God is a process characteristic of Protestantism generally. According to such ministers as Robert Cleaver, rector of Drayton, Oxfordshire in 1598, "hearts must bee crushed and broken," for "till the heart bee broken for sinne, there can be no plaine confession of sinne, and therefore no repentance."[22] The same spiritual state is described by the influential Calvinist, William Perkins, fellow of Christ's College, whose words may have troubled the young Marlowe. Perkins describes the state of "holy desperation" felt by the truly penitent before they throw themselves on the mercy of God. Even among the elect lapses of faith or "spiritual desertions" are common: "This sorte of desertions, though it bee but for a time, yet no part of a Christian man's life is free from them; and very often taking deepe place in the heart of man, they are of long continuance."[23]

Since feelings of despair were familiar to the English Protestants of Shakespeare's day and even considered necessary for salvation, the manifestations of this spiritual state were well demonstrated in contemporary literature. As we have seen, its negative power is dramatized in Marlowe's *Doctor Faustus*. In the words of its hero: "My heart is hardened, I cannot repent," and, in consequence, he realizes: "damned art thou, Faustus, damned; despair and die!" For other characters, however, despair can revive hope by taking away everything but what is ultimately the only essential—trust in God alone. Unlike Faustus, those predestined to be saved will progress from despair to arrive at true repentance, forgiveness, and the remission of sins. This is the process dramatized in Edgar's treatment of his father in *King Lear*. Gloucester must be brought to understand the need to trust in divine providence—"thy life's a miracle"—and to believe that heaven alone determines the timing and conditions of our arrival and departure, our "coming hither" as well as our "going hence."[24] This distinctively Protestant attitude toward the benefits of despair provides a context for analyzing the behavior and intentions of the curious ruler of Vienna in *Measure for Measure*, one who "would have dark deeds darkly answered."[25] Moreover, raising questions of Protestant theology in connection with this work is especially appropriate, for in no other play of Shakespeare's do the "central characters evoke specific biblical passages and theological concepts to explain their crucial deeds; in no other are the allusions so prominent; in no other do they define so distinct and consistent a pattern. . . . This is Shakespeare's most theological play."[26]

If not the central figure, Duke Vincentio is surely the moving force of the action in *Measure for Measure*. Although the deceptions and deceits by which he operates have aroused considerable criticism and complaint, his motives seem generally straightforward.[27] On some occasions at least, his behavior is unambiguous and laudable. By feigning absence from his city, he can test the character of his deputy, Angelo; by using the bedtrick and replacing Isabella with Mariana, Angelo's former fiancée, the Duke can order Angelo to marry her; and by substituting Ragozine, a notorious pirate who died of a "cruel fever," for Claudio, Isabella's brother, the Duke can save the young man's life.

But Duke Vincentio's actions and intervention are not so easily understood in every instance. In fact, a number of times he says and does things that strike one as irrational or perverse. In particular, he seems nearly obsessed with teaching men to confront their death.[28] It is a lesson he repeats almost compulsively. He lectures Claudio on the need to "be absolute for death" (III.i.5)—even eavesdropping to learn if his sermon has been effective—and he does not leave until Claudio is, in the Duke's words, "resolved to die." The Duke also intends to deal with the drunken prisoner Barnardine to "persuade this rude wretch willingly to die." (IV.iii.80) And, before the Duke is through with him, Angelo, too, says he is very ready to end his life: "I crave death more willingly than mercy; / 'Tis my deserving, and I do entreat it." (V.i.474–75)

Moreover, the Duke's eccentricities are evident not only in these examples of his meddling but also in his treatment of Isabella. In this case his explanation for his treatment of her appears cruel, if not almost incomprehensible. Although one may not approve, one can understand that he keeps from her the truth of her brother's fate in order to test her capacity to forgive Angelo: will she join Mariana and plead for the deputy's life even when Isabella believes him responsible for her brother's death? But Duke Vincentio's expressed motive for deceiving her, verbalized in soliloquy, is, in the judgment of Philip Edwards, an "appalling justification."[29] According to what he tells us, the Duke "will keep her ignorant of her good, / To make her heavenly comforts of despair / When it is least expected." (IV.iii.104–8) For Edwards, "God works in mysterious ways, but this beats all—willingly to cause despair in order to show the beauty of divine consolation." Other students of this play also express irritation with the Duke's behavior. Harriett Hawkins finds his action "so patronising as to be more infuriating, in intent, than satisfying when dramatically realized."[30] And Richard A. Levin thinks that when the Duke claims he will make "heavenly comforts of despair," his "rationale seems strained, his cruelty sadistic."[31] The reaction of these critics to the Duke's words is quite understandable, for if his language is divorced from its theological meaning then the comic intrigues that will result in a happy ending—"the beauty of divine consolation"—cannot be reconciled with the notion of providential intervention into human affairs that is also being implied here—"willingly to cause despair." To quote Edwards once more, "The distance between the contrivances necessary for the fulfillment of the comedy and the workings of God which they are meant to suggest is impossibly great."[32] In effect, the concept of the fortunate fall does not usually include the notion that Providence takes as much delight in chastising humanity as in saving it.

Yet by appreciating that despair can lead to positive spiritual growth we may be better able to explain the Duke's course of action. And we should recall that at this point in the play the Duke, now dressed as a friar, may well be providing some religious instruction by what he does. His insistence on the "comforts of despair" expresses what he has in mind since, as we have seen, Protestant theology in particular considered despair a necessary first step to attaining a state of grace.

Regarded in this context, the Duke-as-friar tests the spiritual health of each of the principal characters in the play, acting the part of religious teacher. First in his interview with Juliet, Claudio's pregnant fiancée, he questions her spiritual state to "try [her] penitence, if it be sound / Or hollowly put on." (II.iii.22–23) According to the *Homily* "Of Repentance, and of True Reconciliation unto God," true contrition is "an inward sorrow and grief ... conceived in the heart for the heinousness of sin," and characterized by the willing acceptance of punishment.[33] Recognizing the offensiveness of sin to God, Juliet would "gladly learn" the way to proper contrition. The Friar approves of her resolution, combining repentance and acceptance, moved more by love than fear. The state of her conscience reflects her concern for

her spiritual condition rather than for her self-image or her reputation in the world: "I do repent me as it is an evil, / And take the
shame with joy." (II.iii.35–36) "Her response . . . assures him
that her sorrow is truly contrite, and he leaves with the words,
'There rest.' " (II.iii.36)[34]

Next he turns to Claudio in an effort to make him understand
that peace can be achieved only through the same combination
of repentance and acceptance.[35] Claudio thinks he has learned
the friar's lesson: "To sue to live, I find I seek to die, / And seeking death, find life. Let it come on." (III.i.42–43) But his willingness to "let it come on" is difficult to sustain. When Isabella tells
him that Angelo has offered to exchange Claudio's life for her
chastity, Claudio remembers that "death is a fearful thing," and
he pleads with his sister to save him by yielding to the deputy.[36]
Once more the Duke must urge Claudio to become reconciled
to his plight: "Do not satisfy your resolution with hopes that are
fallible." (III.i.167–68) And once more a resigned Claudio will
seek for pardon: "I am so out of love with life, that I will sue to be
rid of it." Through the Duke's efforts, Isabella's brother "most
willingly humbles himself to the determination of justice" and
has "discredited" the "many deceiving promises of life."
(III.ii.237–41) Having been brought to this positive state of despair, Claudio is ready for the rebirth that will be enacted in the
final scene of the play.

With the prisoner Barnardine, "a man that apprehends death
no more dreadfully but as a drunken sleep," who is both "insen-
sible of mortality, and desperately mortal," the ruler of Vienna
has a more difficult time. His offers of comfort and prayer are
rejected out of hand, and with comic determination Barnardine
swears he "will not die today for any man's persuasion." To
spare him from damnation, Barnardine's jailors grant the Duke-
cum-friar more time so that he can "persuade this rude wretch
willingly to die." Although we watch Duke Vincentio effectively
lead some souls onto the path of salvation, we are never wit-
nesses of his success in this instance. After all, not everyone will
despair, not everyone will seek comfort, and not everyone, ultimately, will be saved; in truth, Barnardine seems rather one of
those "unfit to live or die." The final resolution for the Duke in
the closing moments of the play is to offer Barnardine pardon for

his crimes on earth, extending to him the utmost mercy and leaving him to make his own peace with heaven.

Unlike his failure with Barnadine, the Duke causes Angelo to experience a series of emotional states that ultimately affect his spiritual well-being. Although a man of conscience and moral awareness, Angelo has yielded to the temptations of lust and power. Forced to confront the painful truths of his actions, he suffers from both shame and guilt; these emotions lead him to a new sense of self and enable him to have his turn at the positive aspects of despair. His feelings of sorrow, regret, self-hatred, and repentance leave him in his own self-estimation deserving death: "I am sorry that such sorrow I procure, / And so deep sticks it in my penitent heart / That I crave death more willingly than mercy; / 'Tis my deserving, and I do entreat it." (V.i.472–75) This acknowledgment of his guilt and worthlessness is preparatory to his reformation, a necessary preliminary to his realization that salvation can be attained only through acceptance and faith.

Publicly admitting his guilt and still believing himself responsible for Claudio's death, Angelo has now arrived at the point where his character can be reformed: "No longer session hold upon my shame, / But let my trial be mine own confession. / Immediate sentence, then, and sequent death / Is all the grace I beg." (V.i.369–72) In his spiritual state he can only turn to God with absolute dependence on his mercy; like Claudio, he must learn that salvation arrives through despair. As the Duke says, "your evil quits you well."

In the same final scene, the Duke determines that Lucio, the slanderer and wastrel, is to be put to death after he has been married to "one whom he begot with child," a judgment that recalls Claudio's original plight as well as the Duke's sentence on Angelo before the intercession of Mariana and Isabella. Lucio's life like Angelo's will be spared by the pleas of a woman who loves him, Kate Keepdown; and by confronting his own death, Lucio, too, will be granted the opportunity to be reborn to a new and reformed life.

The positive aspects of despair are fostered by Duke Vincentio not only in the the men but also in Isabella, whose development is carefully monitored by him. The men in the play must be brought to confront their own end, but in her case Isabella must confront the deaths of others. Believing her brother executed at Angelo's order, she must respond to the Duke's sentence of "An Angelo for Claudio, death for death." The severity of this command reflects something of the harshness of her attitudes in the early scenes—her desire for even greater strictness among the nuns of her convent, her prudishness at sexuality, her intolerance for human frailty. The Isabella of the first half of the play might well be expected to approve of the justice of "death for death;" in Mary Lascelles's words, "There is a singular rigidity in her bearing."[37]

Yet by the end of the play Isabella supports Mariana's plea for mercy and argues that Angelo should be spared. Like her brother and the deputy, Isabella has reached a new understanding of life, and like them she has grown under the tutelage of the Duke. For one "in probation of a sisterhood," she has had to deal directly with some of the more seamy aspects of human relations, exactly those furthest removed from her fastidious and reserved nature. As a result, her sympathy for the frailty of humankind and her realization of the need to trust completely in heaven have increased. The change in her character has not come easily or readily. The modest Isabella has "with whispering and most guilty diligence . . . twice o'er" (IV.i.38–40) had to rehearse the arrangements for her promised assignation with Angelo in his garden, and, although the scheme is of the Duke's inventing, she must ask Mariana to meet Angelo in her place. Then, for reasons that the Duke never makes clear and even against her own instincts—"To speak so indirectly I am loath"— Isabella must publicly admit to committing "what I abhor to name," "a vice that most I do abhor:"

> the vile conclusion
> I now begin with grief and shame to utter.
> He would not, but by gift of my chaste body
> To his concupiscible intemperate lust,
> Release my brother; and after much debatement
> My sisterly remorse confutes mine honour,
> And I did yield to him.
>
> (V.i.98–104)

The shame and embarrassment of her situation are compounded, for the Duke, sitting in judgment, rejects her accusation and orders her to prison.

As in his treatment of Claudio and Angelo, Duke Vincentio's intention in all of this is constant: he has told Isabella that her experience is "a physic / That's bitter to sweet end." (IV.v.7–8) He has repeatedly encouraged her: "Show your wisdom, daughter, / In your close patience" and, rather than give way to anger, "give your cause to heaven." (IV.iii.117, 124) His instruction and her experience have clearly taken root, for Isabella as she is arrested expresses the kind of trust in Providence that the Duke nurses out of the far side of despair:

> O you blessed ministers above,
> Keep me in patience, and with ripen'd time
> Unfold the evil which is here wrapped up
> In countenance!
> (V.i. 118–21)

As Darryl Gless explains, "the Duke's manipulations of Isabella result in a loss of all hope in worldly aid and a consequent real and utter dependence on divine ordinance."[38]

This complete trust in heaven to resolve matters that are beyond the power of men to understand or control is the positive outcome of despair: to use Duke Vincentio's own words, "Do not satisfy your resolution with hopes that are fallible." Instead, one must rely on faith alone, a faith that is both tested and strengthened by despair. In the words of Richard Hooker:

> Too much honey doth turn to gall; and too much joy even spiritually would make us wantons. Happier a great deal is that man's case, whose soul by inward desolation is humbled, than he whose heart is through abundance of spiritual delight lifted up and exalted above measure.[39]

From one point of view, Shakespeare dramatizes how the chief characters in this play, following different paths, all arrive at a point where they despair of their own powers. Stripped of all earthly assurance, they must learn to trust in heaven to achieve positive spiritual growth, to become in Hooker's words "happier a great deal." Only by experiencing despair can they receive

those "heavenly comforts" that come when "least expected."
Through the good offices of the Duke, the action of *Measure for Measure* traces this spiritual progress.

Such a positive Church of England reading can be fitted onto the play, but a very different interpretation can also be reasonably argued, for the evidence is highly ambiguous. The positive reading, for example, does not explain why the Duke's actions should be so clumsy and involve such near-misses. Nor does it justify Shakespeare's creation of Lucio, who serves only to undermine the Duke's authority. Nor does it make clear why the murderer Barnardine, who never despairs, is spared and freed. Nor does it account for the fact that Angelo's very brief repentance speeches, delivered immediately before and after his marriage, are so unconvincing both times. Nor does it make sense of Isabella's fierce initial reprimand and rejection of her brother or clarify her future by giving us her response to the Duke's proposal. The play's methods of discourse are so indeterminate—so complex, contradictory, and puzzling—that we cannot reach an assured resolution. Ultimately, we find that the psychological complexity of the principal characters raises troubling questions about both their function and motivation, leaving any analysis of the action problematic. By adjusting or ignoring aspects of the work, we can interpret the play by any one of a number of lights—but all of them leave in the dark those aspects of the play that contradict or fail to support the reading imposed on it. Shakespeare's *Measure for Measure* is a fascinating "problem" play because its meaning, intimately bound up with its indeterminate religious bias, is itself problematic, disturbing, and unresolvable.

4

When You See Me You Know Me and *If You Know Not Me You Know Nobody*: Protestantism and Puritan Propaganda

I

Sᴀᴍᴜᴇʟ ʀᴏᴡʟᴇʏ's *ᴡʜᴇɴ ʏᴏᴜ ꜱᴇᴇ ᴍᴇ ʏᴏᴜ ᴋɴᴏᴡ ᴍᴇ* ᴀɴᴅ Thomas Heywood's *If You Know Not Me You Know Nobody*, loosely based on the careers of Henry VIII and Queen Elizabeth, are prime examples of Protestant theater in the early Stuart years. They demonstrate how dramatists—under the guise of presenting a quasi-historical pageant of nationalistic self-congratulation—shaped their story to privilege certain religious practices and beliefs. And since these plays were produced very shortly after James's accession, they served as a reminder to all, English and Scots alike, of the dangers only recently overcome and still threatening their fragile, post-Reformation security. Yet, filled with color and bustle, jingoistic and direct in their appeal, the storyline of these works seems not only innocent but orthodox. Rowley's jumble of historical facts provides a framework for a loosely joined entertainment: rather than offering matter of any greater import or substance, its action seems to stress the foolery of Patch and Will Summers, the clowns of Wolsey and the king.[1] By contrast, Heywood's work seems to present its history fashioned as a form of miracle drama, a saint's life play showing Elizabeth as "a suffering Protestant martyr consoled by her faith and by the people's love."[2]

The two Stuart plays chosen for analysis here are complementary: one attempts to encompass the broad range of principles generally endorsed by English Protestantism; and the second stresses the importance of the Bible in English, an issue of vital

58

concern, especially to the more Puritan-minded members of the audience. And both works were first staged about the time that James took up residence in England.[3] Between 1603 and 1605 Thomas Heywood's play was in the repertory of Queen Anne's company; Rowley's was in the repertory of Prince Henry's company, whose patron was known to be sympathetic to the religious views and politics advocated in the work. Since "Rowley is himself designated on the titlepage 'servant to the Prince' . . . [and] the subject-matter of the play . . . features 'the birth and virtuous life of Edward Prince of Wales,' the play thus takes its place among the documents of expectant anticipation which militant Protestant writers addressed to Prince Henry . . . in the hope of influencing policy."[4] The date of the first production of either of these two plays cannot be precisely determined, but the fact that the theaters were closed during most of 1603 and that both were entered in the Stationers' Register in 1605, points to 1604/5 as the most likely date for their first appearance.[5] In addition, "since a play presenting Henry VIII as its chief character was more likely to be licensed under James than under Henry's daughter," F. P. Wilson speculates, "the likeliest date for the first production [of Rowley's play] . . . is 1604 after the Fortune theatre had reopened on Easter Monday, 9 April."[6]

Plays about the Tudors were surely less risky when they were no longer on the throne, but James's predecessors are dramatized in these works in ways that stress the reasons for their ultimate success. And in both plays their success is ultimately due to their understanding of the threat represented by Catholicism and to their staunch endorsement of Protestantism. By shaping their stories to provide an opportunity to demonstrate the beneficial effects of Protestant influence on the country and its people, these playwrights may well have been responding to tensions created by the behavior of the new king and his consort shortly after they arrived in London.[7] For from the point of view of the Protestant and especially the Puritan community in the capital, the actions of the new royal couple must have seemed troubling indeed, with Queen Anne's behavior particularly distressing. As Judith Spikes has remarked, the new queen "pointedly refused the Anglican Communion at her coronation, sought offices for English Catholics, [and] corresponded warmly with the Spanish infanta. [While for his part,] James . . . became more enigmatic every day," and at the Hampton Court conference (1604) he denied the Puritan ministers' petitions and reconfirmed the authority of the bishops.[8] His response to the petition to strengthen and reform the Church of England was greatly disappointing. All political change is disquieting, but James's English subjects might well have been distressed by this behavior and fearful of the direction the king could impose on his church.

Compounding their sense of uneasiness, many Protestants also found the initial acts of the new monarch's foreign policy as worrisome as his domestic agenda. Among his first official decisions—and one undertaken much to the amazement of King Philip—James cancelled the letters-of-marque that allowed English privateers to attack Spanish shipping. And he followed this by opening peace negotiations with Spain to end a war between their countries that had dragged on since 1585. Agreement was reached rapidly. Despite the opposition of those at home "who argued that Spain was now so weak that one determined blow might crush her forever," despite the offers of Henry IV that France and England should combine against Spain and Austria, and despite the anger of the Dutch who felt abandoned, a treaty was signed in August 1604.[9] In his first moves, the new Stuart king and his consort were hardly providing a positive political climate for the more committed of their Protestant subjects.

II

Although Rowley's *When You See Me You Know Me* is ostensibly a history of the reign of Henry VIII, the king is not, as one might have expected, a great hero who stands against the Pope. Instead, Henry is rather a moody and capricious politician, insecure and highly susceptible to suggestion.

Rowley begins the action well into Henry's reign; at the opening, a very pregnant Jane Seymour is about to give birth.[10] The principal historical events that led up to that moment—the divorce from Henry's first wife and his remarriage and condemnation of Elizabeth's mother—are never treated. Perhaps the issues relating to Anne Boleyn were still too delicate for dramatizing, but in any case, the king is presented here as a loyal Catholic many years after Henry had actually declared himself

"Supreme Head" of the Church in England. Although Rowley presents his play as a history, drawing his material from popular tradition, from the discussion in Foxe's *Book of Martyrs,* and probably from Holinshed, he is hardly restricted by fact. As F. P. Wilson observes, the playwright "flouts chronology with a freedom unusual even in the chronicle plays of his age."[11] Yet his manipulation of fact was neither arbitrary not idiosyncratic.

In part, Rowley may have had aesthetic reasons for choosing to dramatize certain events and not others, or for altering the historical sequence of those events, or for presenting them in a particular way. For example, one might argue that by extending Wolsey's period of influence well beyond his historical years, Rowley might have felt his play would have greater unity of action. But ultimately we must conclude that Rowley selected and shaped his material in order to further the religious themes that were his central concern. Indeed, Rowley's Wolsey is involved in events that occurred some twenty years after the historical Wolsey had died, but Rowley keeps him alive in the play not as a means of unifying the episodic action but rather so that his continual plotting for advancement of the Papacy can demonstrate how the hierarchy and power structure of the Catholic church make it a continuing threat to the independence of England. Another revealing instance of Rowley's cavalier treatment of fact is that Henry receives the title "Defender of the Faith" in the course of the play even though the stage action begins in 1537, some fifteen years after Pope Leo X actually bestowed that honor. And once again, the event is used by Rowley to demonstrate how the concerns of Rome conflict with those of England: the title comes with a request for an army to fight the Turks or a grant of £12,000 "to be disposd, / As his holines thinkes best for their releife." As Henry's fool, Will Summers, is quick to point out, such favors from Rome carry a high price:

> I thought so, I knew twoold be a monnie matter, when
> als done, now thart defender of the faith, the Pope
> will have thee defend everyie thing himself and all.
>   (II.876–78)

And so history is revised to give it a strongly anti-Catholic presentation.

Moreover, the play's two most sympathetic characters, Queen Catherine Parr and Prince Edward, are the most committed Protestants, for they serve to express and defend the principles of their faith. Rowley has managed their speeches so that they cover most of the points particularly significant to the Catholic opposition. Between them, Catherine Parr and Prince Edward manage to attack such practices as selling indulgences, kneeling and praying to saints for intercession, making pilgrimages, believing in purgatory, and using a Latin rather than an English Bible.

All of the dangers of Catholicism are embodied by the villainous Wolsey. When the play opens, he is negotiating a marriage between the aged king of France and Henry's sister, the Lady Mary, in exchange for French support for his candidacy for the Papacy. When these plans for self-advancement fail, Wolsey determines to triple the bribe he has offered the cardinals, and, protective of Rome's interests in England, he sets about mounting the Catholic opposition to Henry's intended marriage to Catherine Parr:

> She is the hope of Luthers heresie:
> If she be Queene, the Protestants will swell,
> And Cranmer, Tutor to the Prince of Wales,
> Will boldly speake gainst Romes Religion,
> But Bishops weele to Court immediately,
> And plot the downfall of these Lutherans.
> (II.1490–95)

Wolsey is also careful to secure the future of his country for Rome. He instructs Princess Mary's tutors to "ply her to the Popes obedience, / And make her hate the name of Protestant," and he plans to purge her sister of any non-Catholic instructors:

> I doe suspect that Latimer and Ridley,
> Chiefe teachers of the faire Elizabeth,
> Are not sound Catholickes, nor friends to Rome,
> If it be so, weele soone remove them all.
> (II.1496–1502)

As the conflict between Catholic and proto-Protestant views intensifies, the argument for the anti-Roman position is made by

Will Summers, Catherine Parr, and the future Edward VI, with his tutor, Cranmer. Wolsey and the two bishops, Bonner and Gardiner, defend Catholic doctrine. For example, when Queen Catherine and Will Summers agree that one should rather have the prayers of the poor than of the Pope, Wolsey remarks that such thoughts are "Heresie," but Will Summers retorts:

> when the Pope is at [his] best, hee is but Saint Peters debutie [sic], but the poore, present Christ, and therefore should be something better regarded. . . . Would the King wood whip thee and all the Popes whelpes out of England once, for betweene yee, yee have rackt and puld it so, we shal be all poore shortly.[12]
>
> (II.1614–21)

Troubled by the growing religious tensions—"This Land ye know stands wavering in her Faith, / Betwixt the Papists and the Protestants"—Prince Edward asks Cranmer whether purgatory exists. Cranmer argues the Protestant view: "what should neede a third place to containe, / A world of Infinites so vast and mayne." (II.2026–27)

The play also tries to point out the political dangers of obedience to Rome. In a dispute with the bishops, Queen Catherine reasons that the Pope has no higher authority than the king, for both are "Gods Deputie." She also voices the argument that submission to Rome places one's loyalty to the secular ruler in doubt: "How are ye faithfull subjects to the King, / When first ye serve the Pope then after him?" And at this point she goes on to question the validity of those Catholic practices most criticised by Protestants:

> Pray tell the King then, what Scripture have yee,
> To teach religion in an unknowne language?
> Instruct the ignorant to kneele to Saints,
> By bare-foote pilgrimage to visite shrines,
> For money to release from Purgatorie,
> The vildest villaine, theefe, or murderer,
> All this the people must beleeve you can,
> Such is the dregs of Romes religion.
>
> (II.2253–60)

Recognizing that her influence over the king severely threatens their interests, Bonner tells Henry that Catherine and those who would alter the religion of the land "scarcely love your roy-all person," for they "disturbe the state." (I.2283). The solution is simple: "The Queene deare Lord must be removed from you."

To strengthen this point, Gardiner reminds the king of the rebellion fomented by Wycliff's followers and, as proof that Catherine's conduct is pernicious, he claims she has been meeting privately with a Lutheran sect in "secret conventickells . . . to wrest the grounds of all religion: / Seeking by tumults to subvert the state."[13] More importantly, he and Bonner claim that this "sect of Lutherans" "conspire against" the life of the king. Henry's fears are roused: he attacks Luther, agrees to have Catherine placed in the Tower, and removes Cranmer as tutor to Edward.

The contrast between Catholic and Protestant beliefs is stressed in the following scene when Prince Edward receives letters from his half-sisters, Mary and Elizabeth. He rejects Mary's advice because she commends him to the Virgin and encourages him "to invocate" the saints as "intermissers" or intermediaries. He would rather heed Elizabeth's words, for she counsels her brother to pray to God who "alone / Can strengthen thee, and confound thine enimies." Elizabeth is his "best beloved," and, meditating on her virtues, Edward determines to pray to God "For preservation, that can himselfe preserve me, / Without the helpe of Saint or cerimonie." (II.2406–8)

And indeed, it is Edward who ultimately defeats the Bishops' plans to have the Queen placed on trial for conspiring to

> . . . raise rebellion in the state,
> Alter religion, and bring Luther in,
> And to new government inforce the king.
> (II.2485–87)

By pleading on bended knees to his father, Edward persuades Henry to hear Catherine. In her defense, she claims that her conversations on religion were undertaken merely as a diversion:

> . . . to wast the time,
> Knowiug as then your grace was weake and sickly,
> So to expell parte of your paine and griefe.
> (II.2670–72)

Moreover, making use of an argument found in Foxe's *Acts and Monuments*, known as the *Book of Martyrs*, Rowley's Queen points out that her "womans wit" is "helde too weake / To maintaine proofes about religion." When Gardiner and Bonner come to arrest her, Henry orders them "as prisoners to the Fleete" instead, but Catherine intervenes and, demonstrating true charity, begs Henry for their pardon.

As the action moves quickly to its joyous ending, Henry learns conclusively that the Catholics and their church are dangerously subversive to his kingdom. Wolsey has stored up treasure in his cellar, intending to bribe his way to the papal throne—something the king long suspected—and Henry and the Emperor Charles discover what Catherine had foreseen, that Wolsey has been a false emissary, serving the will of Rome before the orders of his king. For this and his other crimes and presumptions, the cardinal is dismissed, and Henry now seems to understand that those who claim to be "deputie unto his holinesse" are really "false abusers of religion." The mood is festive, for the play closes with a sense that providence actively intervenes to protect the course of true religion in England. With a stage crowded by heralds, trumpeters, guards, and supernumeraries, the king and his court in full regalia bring the proceedings to an impressive conclusion.

Although his work has grave deficiencies as a chronicle history, Rowley provides enough colorful action to guarantee his play's success—e.g. Henry in disguise, fighting in the streets, arrested and placed in the Counter; the bawdy dialogues of Will Summers and Wolsey's jester, Patch.[14] But the work's chief claim to durability is surely its emphatic treatment of religious issues. Protestant England is portrayed as a type of the Old Testament Israelite nation, saved from the cruel plots of its enemies because it has held to the true faith. And that injunction, put forth in the guise of a quasi-historical pageant play, is the heart of the matter.

III

In contrast to the broad Protestant values of Rowley's play, Heywood's *If You Know Not Me You Know Nobody or the Troubles of Queen Elizabeth* makes a more concerted appeal to Protestant, and especially Puritan, interests by placing particular emphasis on the power and importance of the English Bible; Heywood gives the Scriptures in English the central place in this work that they held especially in the Puritan service. For the Puritans believed that only faith in the English Bible and the active intervention of a Protestant providence had saved Elizabeth and her country from the unrelenting efforts of Rome to retain religious domination over them. And since that danger was still present, vigilance was essential.

Indeed, the two features of Puritan life that particularly distinguished it from other varieties of Protestantism were first, that its followers gave a special prominence to the role of the Bible in English, and second, that they held Protestant beliefs with far greater conviction, more fervor, than their countrymen. As Patrick Collinson points out, "puritanism was not a distinct and coherent philosophy but a tendency . . . and puritans were not a sect on their own but a presence within the Church, believing what other protestants believed, but more intensely. The authority of Scripture was the formal ground of protestant faith, but in puritan circles the language and imagery of the Bible actively permeated every aspect of existence."[15] For these followers of the "godly life" the Bible in English played an especially critical role. To quote once again from the preaching of that influential Cambridge minister William Perkins, the Scriptures were "of sufficient credit in themselves, needing not the testimony of any creature not subject to the censure of either men or angels . . . being the only foundation of our faith and the rule and canon of all truth."[16] Nothing was more important than the Bible. Peter Lake explains that once Protestants rejected all Catholic authority—Pope, church, church fathers, priests—they were

> left with the study of scripture (guided, of course, by properly trained clerics) and the internal testimony of the Spirit attendant upon it as the only source for, and validation of, true belief. This was something which puritans took seriously not merely as a polemical position against Rome but as a guiding principle in their practical divinity.[17]

M. M. Knappen has even argued that for Tudor Puritans, "the Bible was not only the unique authority; it was the complete one."[18] Indeed, "the Bible, either in its explicit teaching or in what one puritan divine calls 'the constant sense of the general tenor of scripture' . . . was the only authority which the puritan acknowledged in matters of religion."[19] In the words of William Haller, for the proper conduct of a religious life and for the achieving of grace "the essential imperative . . . , the one thing not to be omitted, was for everyone the reading of the Bible."[20]

The notion that playwrights might themselves have Puritan leanings or write for a Puritan audience requires some special consideration, for Puritanism, with its strong disapproval of certain amusements and sports, has long been thought inimical to the drama. If that is truly the case, any involvement in the theater seems highly unlikely, and Puritan playgoers sound like a rare breed indeed.[21] But actually, many students of theater history have now come to think that opposition to the drama among moderate Puritans was itself rare. The expensive pageants commissioned to celebrate the investiture of new Lord Mayors of London, an allied form of theatrical endeavor, were subsidized by the incumbents' company, for example the Grocer's or Draper's, whose members might well be practicing Puritans. These spectacles, demonstrating the richness and influence of the underwriting company as well as the glory of England's capital, were often devised by such men as Dekker and Middleton.[22] In effect, then, Lord Mayor's shows were created by Puritans, paid for by Puritans, and performed for Puritans.[23] And Alfred Harbage observed that William Perkins notwithstanding, "the very shrillness of the pulpit attacks upon playgoing suggests frustration."[24] Margot Heinemann has concluded that if we define Puritanism broadly as those wishing to cleanse the English church of Popery or to worship according to a purified service:

> it seems that a great part of the London popular audience, and a number even among the 'select' audience and great court patrons of the drama, could be included within the Puritan spectrum.[25]

Moreover, whenever plays are acted to generate an income, writers and performers will sooner or later create the type of stage entertainment that will attract an audience.[26] If, in addition, the content of these plays has the potential either of consolidating public opinion or of influencing the power structure, they offer an added incentive to those who would perform them. For these reasons we should not be surprised that an Elizabethan-Jacobean Protestant or Puritan-oriented drama appeared, directly reflecting the attitudes of those who wished to affect government policy. Indeed in his study of Tudor drama and politics David Bevington proved just how closely theater and religion were related.[27]

So basic aspects of Protestantism that were especially valued by Puritanism—fervent commitment to a life instructed by the Bible—emerge so clearly stressed in some popular plays that they can not be missed; once again, the message itself evidently remained so orthodox that there was no reason for censorship. Yet it may not be without significance that as a continuing theme these points reappeared in a number of dramas written during the early years of James's rule—perhaps in the hope that the new monarch would heed this message. In these works the prominence and value given to the English Bible as well as the emphasis on its importance in fulfilling the national destiny clearly reflect the Protestant/Puritan sympathies of the authors and very probably of the audiences for whom they were writing.

Although the events of *If You Know Not Me* trace "The Troubles of Queene Elizabeth," as the subtitle indicates, the real subject of the play is the religion of the realm, the very subject James has reopened with the Hampton Court Conference. And since the action of Heywood's work stresses the importance of the English Bible, the play has a strong Puritan bias. When it opens we learn that the Protestant-inspired revolt of Wyatt and the Kentish rebels against their new Catholic queen, Mary Tudor, has been defeated. Two of the queen's archcatholic supporters, Gardiner, the bishop of Winchester, and Sir Henry Beningfield, implicate Elizabeth, "a favorite of these heritiques," as a confederate in Wyatt's rebellion and as an instigator of the Suffolk petition for the right of individual conscience. Meanwhile Mary, further prompted by her Catholic advisors, has little memory of her promise to her loyal Protestant subjects. Although she had told them they "Should still enjoy [their] consciences, and use that faith / Which in king Edwards dayes was held Canonicall" (II.84–85), now that the revolt has been put down, she is determined "they shall learne t'obay." Dodds, the bearer of the petition from the Suffolk men, is ordered to the pillory for three days, and Elizabeth is to be escorted to London under armed guard to answer her accusers. Even the princess's supporters are harshly dealt with, being either dismissed from court or placed in the Tower. Clearly, Heywood makes Mary's policy appear tyrannical:

> Mary: Away with him, ile teach him know his place,
> To frowne when we frowne, smile on whome we grace.
> Winch: Twilbe a meanes to keepe the rest in awe,
> Making their soveraignes brow to them a lawe.
>
> (II.122–25)

After these opening scenes of some 150 lines that serve as prologue, we are introduced to the heroine, who embodies the hope of the Protestant cause. An experienced playwright, Heywood knows the advantages both of delaying Elizabeth's entrance to increase audience anticipation and of preparing for her sympathetic reception by the dialogue that immediately precedes her appearance. The princess Elizabeth is described as "wondrous crazey," "all unquiet," and "giddy with continuall griefe," and we first see her propt up in her bed, suffering with illness, faint and sorrowful. Though her doctors report that moving her is "not deadly, but yet dangerous," she agrees reluctantly to obey her sister's orders and leave for Westminster—"no soule more glad then I, / To doe my duty to her Majestie." To allow for the lapse of time required for Elizabeth's removal to London, Mary and King Philip of Spain are shown establishing their Catholic wedding plans—"This shalbe Spanish England, ours English Spaine." The incident is sufficient to distress any Englishman of Heywood's time.

In her suffering Elizabeth is portrayed as a kind of Protestant saint, demonstrating the qualities of piety and holiness valued by puritans. The young princess appears surrounded by her former household officers, now dismissed and weeping, who proclaim her innocence: "so good a ladie & so beautifull, so absolute a mistris, / And perfect." She, however, remains steadfast in her faith: "All that heaven sends is welcome," she maintains. Yet her remarks are not without a degree of self-pity, faintly recalling something of Shakespeare's language in *Richard II*.

> I am now a prisoner; and shall want nothing,
> I have some friends about her majesty,

That are providing for mee all things; all things;
I, even my grave; and being possest of that,
I shall need nothing: weepe not I pray,
Rather you should rejoyce:
If I miscarry in this enterprise, and aske you why,
A Virgine and a Martyr both I dy.

                                        (II.335–42)

But unlike Richard, who indulges himself in his sorrow, Elizabeth, learning that her friends have been dismissed from court,
stalwartly places her trust in God, who "will helpe, deliver, save,
defend the just." Confronted by her hostile examiners, Elizabeth
kneels before them: "to the Queene in you I bend my knee." As
she intended, they find her action disconcerting. When Gardiner,
speaking for his colleagues, asks if she judges them harshly, Elizabeth responds ambiguously:

Knowe you your owne guilt my good Lord Chancelor,
That you accuse your selfe, I thinke not so,
I am of this mind, no man is my foe.

                                        (II.374–76)

Elizabeth accepts her sister's authority, but she refuses to
"submit;" that is, to acknowledge she was in any way involved
in the opposition to Mary's coronation. And her examiners, having no evidence, can only threaten and bluster—"the Queene
must here you sing another song." While they briefly clear the
stage to determine how to deal with her obstinacy, Elizabeth offers a prayer for divine protection "from these ravening Jawes, /
That hidious death presentes by Tyrants Lawes."

As a means of giving voice to public sentiment and heightening
his sympathetic portrait of Elizabeth, Heywood shows her being
transferred to the Tower, under the orders of Mary's counsel-
lors. Three of the soldiers who are to escort her to her new residence comment obliquely on her character and on the
government's policy. In their mind she is a "vertuous Princesse"
and since the reason for her imprisonment is not known, "knav-
ery" may be suspected.

By dramatizing the harsh and unjust treatment of Elizabeth,
Heywood points up the cruelty and untrustworthiness of the

Catholics. And even as he presents their actions negatively, Heywood reveals more and more the positive Protestant and even Puritan bias of the action by emphasizing the importance and power of the Bible in English. When Elizabeth is removed to the Tower, forced to enter her prison through Traitor's Gate (thus implying her guilt and justifying her confinement), she finds her sole comfort and protection is her English Bible.

> On this cold stone I sit, raine in my face,
> But better heere, than in a worser place
> Where this bad man will lead me.
> Clarentia, reach my booke, now leade me where you please
> From sight of day; or in a dungeon I shall see to pray.
>
> (II.604–8)

As punishment for her obstinacy in matters of religion, Elizabeth is badly treated, denied "the priviledge / Of any walke, or garden," access to fresh air, or attendance by her personal servants. Her suffering proves her strength of character as well as the depth of her religious commitment: by the end of the scene when her gentleman-usher delivers a prayer for her safety Elizabeth has assumed the role of spiritual and political leader of all anti-Catholics. Since her English prayer book is the basis for her faith and salvation, the Catholics hope to deny her access to it:

> But that my warrant is not yet so strict,
> Ide lay her in a dungeon where her eyes,
> Should not have light to read her prayer booke,
> So would I danger both her soule and body,
> Cause she an alyen is to us catholiques,
> Her bed should be all snakes, her rest dispayre,
> Torture should make her curse her faithles prayer.
>
> (II.717–23)

Even her enemies recognize that Elizabeth's English Bible is not only essential for the practice of her religion but the source of her spiritual and physical protection.

Help for Elizabeth comes from an unexpected quarter, for Philip of Spain, although a devout Catholic, is a better politician than his coreligionists in Mary's court. Once he is informed of her condition, he orders better treatment for Elizabeth. Unlike the fanatical Catholics around him, Philip understands that a successful union of his country and England requires popular support, and that Elizabeth can be useful in swaying public opinion. Perhaps the playwright is also suggesting that Spain and its ruler are no longer so dangerous to England as her own enemies at home—a position supporting James's new peace with Spain and encouraging the new king to favor the more moderate wing of the Church of England party in the Hampton Court Conference.

With their efforts to torment Elizabeth blocked by Philip, Gardiner and the archcatholic faction now arrange for Elizabeth to be placed in the care of their agents, Beningfield and his man, Barwick. Yet the common people show their love for the princess by giving her nosegays, lining her way, and ringing church bells. When asked to describe her state, Elizabeth cleverly replies, "Tamquam Ovis," i.e., like a lamb to slaughter. With these words she is able to make the audience aware both of her astute political instincts and of the grave danger she faces from Beningfield. And to broaden the canvas and illustrate the general troubles that will follow a Spanish/English alliance, an anonymous Englishman and Spaniard quarrel in the street; they duel, and the Spaniard unfairly kills the Englishman. Philip, realizing the gravity of what has happened, orders his own countryman put to death and resolves to make Mary and Elizabeth friends. Again, Spain is not so great a threat to English security as the danger of falling away from the practice of true religion.

In scene fourteen, the climax of the play when Elizabeth's life is directly threatened, the essential importance of the English Bible is made absolutely clear. For here, unexpectedly, Heywood adopts the staging methods of the Catholic mystery play for Protestant and Puritan purposes. Left in the hands of Beningfield and Barwick, Elizabeth feels certain she will die. While she sleeps a dumb show is enacted. The Catholic faction—Gardiner, the constable of the Tower, Barwick, and Friars—enter at one door, and the Friars offer to kill the sleeping young woman. But two angels who enter from the opposite door drive the murderous Catholics back. Then an "angel opens the Bible, and puts it in her hand as she sleepes." When Elizabeth arises refreshed, she discovers the Scriptures placed in her arms and takes this as an act of heavenly inspiration that "will guide the just." Further consolation comes from the fact that her English Bible is opened to the verse: "Whoso putteth his trust in the Lord / Shall not be confounded." According to Katherine McLuskie, the emphasis in this scene is on "the combination of magic and superstition which was at the heart of popular religion."[28] Elements of that combination, intended to produce a response of awe and wonder, may be here, but surely Heywood's main purpose is in demonstrating as strenuously as possible the power of the English Bible as the basis of the true faith, a faith that will protect and preserve the realm.

Proof of the power of the true faith is offered again in the next scene where an active providence serves Protestant ends. Attending at court, Sir Thomas Gresham waits to have his business contract sealed. But Gardiner and the Lord Constable are so intent on hiding Elizabeth's death warrant among the papers to be signed by Philip that they allow Gresham to overhear their plans. Gresham thanks heaven for making him "a willing instrument her life to save." He leaves for help, returning with Lord Howard, who is able to stop Philip from signing the order in error; once again, the danger is not from Spain, but from the English who undermine their own true faith. Gardiner, his plans now discredited, admits that such an outcome proves Elizabeth's life "is guarded by the hand of heaven." Once more Heywood has shown us that a Protestant deity rewards those who trust in him.

And that lesson is repeated just as forcefully in the closing scenes of the play. By remaining stalwart and trusting that God will keep his promise "to raise them frends that on his word relie," Elizabeth succeeds in overcoming Mary's doubt and hostility. Their reconciliation delights Philip, who must return to Spain. When Gardiner, ailing, hopes to try one more time to incense the queen, he is again defeated by the hand of heaven. In the final dumb show we witness the parting of Philip, the death of Gardiner, and the installation of Cardinal Pole as chancellor. Then in short order we learn not only that Pole "is sodenly falne sicke and like to die" but also that the queen, whether in sorrow from Philip's leaving, Gardiner's death, or Pole's illness, is herself "exceeding sick."

Now the play moves to a triumphant conclusion. Elizabeth is distressed by a dream, but shortly Sir Henry Carey arrives to inform her that she is the new monarch. He is followed by others bearing the good news. The citizens, having little thought for their newly deceased ruler, prepare to build bonfires "for joy of the newe Queene," and to the sound of trumpets the procession leads the new ruler to London. Elizabeth appoints her court officers, and "praysing that King that all Kings els obay," she shows mercy, justice, and wisdom in her treatment of the constable and Beningfield. After a second trumpet fanfare and a turn about the stage, the procession is greeted by the mayor of London, who presents Elizabeth with a purse and, what is clearly valued even more highly, an English Bible.

The new monarch properly understands the importance of this gift—Elizabeth refers to it as the "true food," that can save souls, the "Anchor [of] every soule," and "the fountaine cleere imaculate." Her paean of appreciation, stressing the essential quality of the English Bible for the practice of true religion, expresses a view of Protestantism that is deeply colored by Puritan sympathies. First kissing the book and commending it as the pathway to honor and bliss, as a source of solace, and of bodily and spiritual care, Elizabeth pledges to make the English Bible "so long shut up, so long hid" free and open for her people now and in the future.

> That happy issue that shall us succeed,
> And in our populous Kingdome this booke read:
> For them as for our owne selves we humbly pray,
> They may live long and blest. . . .
>   (II.1578–98)

By closing the play with a stirring tribute to Protestant truth and with a pledge to maintain the English Bible as the keystone of faith, Heywood leaves his audience in no doubt about its message.[29] Moreover, the conclusion of his play could only encourage spectators to contrast the very recent behavior of the new king and queen with that of their former ruler on the occasion of her accession. Elizabeth clearly knew how to work a public assembly; her love of attention and of displays of mass affection were markedly different from her cousin's reactions, for well known among his failings as a public figure was his terror of crowds.

Indeed, Heywood has based his dramatization on an actual

event in Elizabeth's coronation procession in 1559. Although he
has the Lord Mayor present the English Bible to the queen in his
play, in fact when her procession reached the Little Conduit in
Cheapside the English Bible was passed to the queen through a
child who represented Truth. "When her Grace understood that
the Bible in English should be delivered unto her by Truth . . .
she thanked the city for that gift and said that she would often-
times read over that book."[30] Taking full advantage of the occasion, "as soon as she had received the booke, [Elizabeth] kissed
it, and with both her handes held up the same, and so laid it upon
her brest, with great thankes to the cittie therefore."[31] The effect
was, of course, "to the great comfort of the lookers on."[32] In contrast, Elizabeth's successor could not manage to conceal his dis-
comfort and impatience with the slowness of his coronation
procession in 1604 as it moved through the city, and Queen
Anne's refusal to take the Anglican communion during the cere-
mony could only distress all their Protestant subjects. By reminding Londoners of their recent past and implying a contrast
with their new monarch, Heywood makes his audience of
1604–5 even more aware of the greatness of the falling off.

IV

Both Heywood's and Rowley's work went through many editions. For example, *When You See Me* was reprinted four times
and *If You Know Not Me*, eight.[33] Not only do the number of printings attest to the plays' continuing appeal but the dates of the
printings also suggest that Heywood's work in particular may
have been reissued in response to important moments in the conflict between Protestant and Catholic interests. For example, the
first edition (1605) followed shortly after the peace with Spain
and the Hampton Court conference that left many Protestants
and most Puritans dissatisfied with their new monarch. The second printing (1613) followed hard upon the government's alliance with the German Protestant princes and the death of
Prince Henry. The third appeared (1621) when, with the death
of King Philip III of Spain, the marriage negotiations of Prince
Charles with the infanta were reexamined; as a part of these proceedings Rome promised a papal dispensation enabling the in-

fanta to marry Charles only on condition that English Catholics would be guaranteed complete freedom of worship. And the last edition (1632) came off the presses at the time that Laud was consolidating his power to enforce conformity in religious practices and, as we shall discuss below, the death of Frederick, the elector Palatine and king of Bohemia, left Charles's popular sister Elizabeth a widow.[34]

Whether or not particular historical events provided the incentive for some or all of these editions, the continued reprinting of these two plays for more than twenty-five years clearly attests to their popularity with the London public. The reasons for this popularity are not difficult to determine. Both works would serve those interested in furthering the Protestant cause on the one hand by reminding the Stuart monarchs of the religious preferences of the people and on the other hand by consolidating public support for Protestantism. According to Margot Heinemann, "There is here a sizeable element of nostalgia for a golden past, only partly mythical, in which relations between Crown and City were based on deep mutual respect and trust, and Elizabeth's England was the terror of Spain. [But] by 1605 . . . there had been a real change of relations between monarch and merchant, monarch and citizens, compared with 1588."[35] And that change continued with the gap between the two growing wider. Indeed, among the more committed Protestants the feeling of disillusionment with the Stuart government grew ever stronger under the pressure of the political/religious antagonisms sweeping Europe. Even the transfer of power from James to Charles was insufficient for the theater to call up a more positive image of the ruling government. As Martin Butler explains, the fact that an Elizabethan theatrical style could persist even in the refined atmosphere of the Caroline court "suggests that the attitudes on which they were founded—their traditional and highly-charged popular sympathies and values—were still felt to be strongly relevant to England in the 1630s."[36]

Butler points out that stage presentations of their Tudor predecessors cast the early Stuart monarchs in a poor light. Heywood's *If You Know Not Me*, acted at the Phoenix, attests to the powerful idea derived from Foxe's *Book of Martyrs* that Elizabeth, steadfast in her faith, withstood her enemies and oppressors:

finally entering triumphantly into her rule, English Bible in hand....
This play, in its eighth edition in 1639, was plainly one of the most
popular of its age, and perhaps Rowley's companion piece on Henry
VIII's merry japes, Wolsey's dismissal and the godly education of
Edward VI, *When You See Me You Know Me* (1604), which reached
its fourth edition in 1632, was still being performed alongside it. If so,
it must have been an astonishing spectacle in Charles's London to
see Elizabeth and Henry striding the indoor stages as . . . icons of
good princes piously furthering the gospel whose presence implicitly
damned a king who had failed to further the continuing process of
reform and preaching the gospel which Foxe demanded.[37]

Under the pretense of staging the past, these plays continually
called attention to the difficulties of the present—the growing
problem of royal finances and court behavior, the misguided direction of Stuart policies in international politics, and what was
regarded as the indecisiveness of the monarchy's position on
matters of religion.[38] The events enacted in these plays stress the
dangers of the Catholic conspiracy, the courage of such queens
as Elizabeth and Catherine Parr to hold to the paths of true god-
liness, and even the role of Providence in saving England from
subservience to Rome. Catherine is able to argue her case with
Henry only because the bill of accusations against her fortu-
itously falls into the hands of one of her supporters in sufficient
time, and angels intervene to protect the sleeping Princess Elizabeth from those who intend to murder her. But naturally, one
cannot always count on divine intervention or on the wisdom of
rulers whose actions stand in marked contrast with those of their
predecessors. Under the label of chronicle history, both works
teach their audience that the practices of the true faith can only
be preserved by public vigilance, determination, and fortitude.
Surely these plays were performed and printed as a deliberate
attempt to unify the efforts and resolve of those who supported
the religious practices they advocated even as they billed themselves as light entertainments dramatizing England's past.

5

Bartholomew Fair and Jonsonian Tolerance

I

By the time *BARTHOLOMEW FAIR* WAS STAGED IN 1614, BEN Jonson understood from more firsthand experience than most of his fellow playwrights the dangers of writing for the stage. The bitter memories of his entanglement with the authorities over *The Isle of Dogs* (1597), *Poetaster* (1601), *Sejanus* (1603), and *Eastward Ho* (1605) would have taught him the importance of subtlety and discretion when touching on matters of church and state. As a consequence, Jonson and his colleagues developed strategies of indirection and allusion, of ambiguity and suggestion, of hinting through seemingly trivial facts to accomplish what Martin Butler, to quote his fine phrase once again, called "signaling according to cautious codes."[1] By using such "signals," a playwright might hope to stay out of trouble, for these were the ways that he could imply meaning, enabling him to express himself on subjects that, though potentially dangerous to handle, were of intense concern; one of these, it seems, was the changed nature of the Jacobean court and its acceptance of Roman Catholics.

With this in mind, we might question why in *Bartholomew Fair* Jonson chooses to emphasize what seems to be a minor detail: that Bartholomew Cokes and his tutor, Humphrey Wasp, come from Harrow on the Hill. After all, through reiteration, an unimportant fact can be suspected of functioning as a clue to a larger or covert meaning; what at first looks innocuous can prove to be highly suggestive, giving a work a new coloration or altering its implications. Moreover, Jonson is a writer who leaves nothing to chance. What might seem to be random or haphazard is never without meaning in his work; as we have come to appreciate, the

Jonsonian universe is truthful, just, and consistent.[2] So we ought to consider why in almost every act of the play the author takes pains to tell us that Cokes is "an esquire of Harrow" and that he and "his man" Wasp have left Harrow to come to the fair. References to this location as their home are repeated often, and one is reminded of the fact periodically. In the very first speech in the play, we learn that "Cokes of Harrow o'th'Hill" has ordered a marriage license to marry Grace Wellborn on St. Bartholomew Day, 24 August, the day when the action is set. (I.i.3)[3] At the midpoint of the play, Wasp, exasperated by Cokes's stupidity, regrets coming to the fair: "Lord send me at home once, to Harrow o'the Hill again, / If I travel any more, call me Coriat; with all my heart." (III.v.213–15) Before he is robbed for the third and final time by Nightingale and Edgworth, Cokes admits that he doesn't "know the way out" of the fair "to go home . . . , 'Dost thou know where I dwell, I pray thee?' " he asks the ballad singer. (IV.ii.23–26) And the matter of his residence is raised one last time when, near the close of the play, Wasp seeks Cokes at the puppet show, describing him as "a tall young squire of Harrow o'the Hill." (V.iv.81)

Perhaps for them, as for other characters in the world of this play, geographical origins can reveal qualities of mind and spirit. For example, the hypocritical Puritan, Rabbi Zeal of the Land Busy, hails from an appropriate location for one so fanatic in his religious persuasion. Rabbi Busy is an ex-baker from Banbury, a town in Oxfordshire closely identified in the public mind with both cakes and Puritan extremism. "A noted haunt of Puritans" is how Herford and the Simpsons describe it in their edition.[4] And Adam Overdo, justice of the peace and judge of the temporary court that administers law at the fair, is a London resident and a stalwart member of the Church of England, though in all honesty he confesses that faulty intelligence has caused him from time to time "to mistake an honest zealous pursuivant for a seminary." (II.i.30–31)[5] As Richard Levin has pointed out, the crucial difference between Busy and Overdo as critics of the fair is not so much "that one represents the church and the other state, . . . or that one is a Puritan and the other an Anglican, but that the Puritan prophet cynically uses his brand of ideology . . . to delude others, while the ideology of the Anglican judge . . . has no other purpose than to delude himself."[6] That is an especially revealing observation, for it suggests not only that this justice may be easily confused—a truth we come to discover for ourselves—but also that one form of Christianity may not be so easily distinguished from another. If Overdo is the representative figure for the Church of England and Busy for the arch-Puritan faction, one a "conscientious Anglican judge" and the other a "fanatical Puritan preacher," as Henry Wells labels them, then Wasp, the third character who later gets placed in the stocks along with them, represents the old religion, that third party of Christians in England, the Catholics.[7]

II

In fact, the association of Harrow on the Hill and covert Catholicism would have been as evident to Jonson's audience as that between Banbury and the Puritans. A convenient seven miles from London, the settlement at Harrow was notorious for its recusants—Catholics who refused to attend Anglican services. Believing in the absolute position of the Pope, they refused to take the Oath of Supremacy to the Crown. As an especially notable example we might consider the infamous Bellamy family whose manor house of Uxendon, Harrow on the Hill, became a center for missionary priests.[8] There and at Preston manor house, also at Harrow, they maintained no little notoriety over a thirty year period. Even into the first decade of the seventeenth century every important Catholic priest or plotter seems to have passed through their care: Edmund Campion was entertained at Uxendon shortly before his arrest in 1581; Richard Bristow, the author of *Motives Inducing to the Catholic Faith*, was a resident in the house for some time; Anthony Babington was captured there in 1586 and the Jesuit Robert Southwell in 1592. The members of the Bellamy family were quite prepared to suffer for their faith. Catherine Bellamy, widowed in the early 1580s, ultimately died in the Tower; her son Jerome was hanged for aiding conspirators; and two other sons died in prison. Another son, Richard, continued the family tradition. In 1587, he, his wife, and two of his sons were indicted for recusancy, and in 1592 his daughter, Anne, imprisoned in the Gatehouse of Westminister, was seduced by Robert Topcliffe, a notorious pursuivant. She was forced to betray . . . Southwell. . . . [Later] Richard and Catherine, charged with receiving 15 or 16 priests, were committed to the Gatehouse. . . . After ten years' "persecutions of extreme barbarity" Richard conformed and was released, selling his Uxendon estates and dying in poverty in Belgium.[9]

The Bellamy-Catholic alliance and their association with Harrow continued into James's reign, for "Catherine Bellamy, widow, late wife of Richard Bellamy," figured in a mortgage of Preston manor house in 1609.[10]

Well before 1609, however, their activities as well as those of other English Catholics were hardly a real threat to the establishment, and many of their coreligionists had found their way into secure positions at court. Indeed, the composition of the Stuart court—the ethnic origins, religious affiliations, and social class of its members—was anything but uniform. Surrounding the king was a "conglomeration of Scots and English, old and new nobility, learned and unlearned, Catholics, Puritan sympathizers, and Established Churchmen, sophisticates and provincials."[11] By 1614 when *Bartholomew Fair* was acted, English Catholics were not a danger to the stability of the government or the crown.

For the better informed members of Jonson's audience, who might have attended *Bartholomew Fair*'s second performance before the king, the issue of the place of Catholic citizens in English society was, in fact, just then receiving some sympathetic attention. And Jonson's portrayal of the fairgoers from Harrow on the Hill would have reinforced these feelings.[12] The subject was one that had long been debated. As Alan Dures has observed,

In the years between 1610 and 1613 foreign affairs, and in particular England's relations with Spain, were an important element in shaping domestic policy. . . . The arrival in August 1613 of . . . Count Gondomar as Spanish ambassador of London signaled a closer relationship between England and Spain. [Under Gondomar's influence] the severity of the persecution [of English Catholics] appears to have lessened after 1613, and there are fewer complaints from the Catholics. [Moreover,] between 1613 and 1621 . . . the vigour of the king's anti-Catholic policy fluctuated, partly in response to relations with Spain, and partly at the personal whim of James.[13]

But in reaction to the increasingly favorable response to English Catholics at court, parliament felt uneasy and feared their growing influence on the king. Parliamentary distrust became so great that "in 1614 Sir Peter Bucke was hauled before Star Chamber for claiming that Northampton and other court Catholics had petitioned the king for a formal toleration for their co-religionists."[14] As a sign of their continued hostility, parliamentary and ecclesiastical authorities continued to impose fines and restrictions on English Catholics despite the opposition of James, like Elizabeth before him. For the more vindictive Anglicans and the more fanatical Puritans, these penalities were all too easy a source of income, and the satisfaction of victimizing Catholics was all too rewarding.[15] In effect, English Catholics were legally and systematically plundered.

Victimization and plundering also describe rather accurately what happens to Bartholomew Cokes as a consequence of his visit to the fair, for he is systematically pillaged throughout the action of the play. In Act 2, Cokes is relieved of his silver purse; in Act 3 his gold purse is stolen along with "Mistress Grace's handkercher, too, out o' the tother pocket;" and in Act 4 he loses his sword, cloak, and hat. One of the thieves remarks of Cokes that like a true martyr of the fair, "a man might cut out his kidneys, I think, and he never feel 'em, he is so earnest at the sport." (IV.ii.39–40) At the end of the play we realize that Cokes is bereft of everything—money, toys, expensive clothes, sword, and even his fiancée. But just possibly in his losses he has also gained an unexpected freedom, for once Cokes has learned that Wasp was put into the stocks, his guardian's moral authority over the young man is over; Wasp knows he "must think no longer to reign, my government is at an end." (V.iv.97–98)

Just as Cokes recalls the situation of English Catholics—who might all break free of Rome—Humphrey Wasp manifests the dogmatism of the Renaissance Catholic hierarchy as it might have looked from the Anglican point of view: an administration that combined absolutism with illogicality and mixed matters of faith with irascibility. Without too much straining one could find in Wasp's language and behavior elements that suggest a parody of a papal edict: "I have no reason, nor I will hear of no reason, nor I will look for no reason, and he is an ass that either knows any or looks for't from me." (IV.iv.39–41) With an exasperated

shout at the proctor John Littlewit, Wasp behaves with characteristic contradiction almost at the moment of his very first appearance in the play: "I know? I know nothing, I. What tell you
me of knowing? Now I am in haste, sir, I do not know, and I will
not know, and I scorn to know, and yet (now I think on't) I will
and do know as well as another." (I.iv.18–21) As Eugene Waith
points out, Wasp is "like Cokes, but for different reasons: his
mind is in such endless motion that there is never time to establish a fixed center. Instead of embracing all the world he rejects
it all, thereby showing no more discrimination than Cokes."[16]
How appropriate that Wasp takes such particular relish in the
game of "vapours"—"every man to oppose the last man that
spoke, whether it concerned him or no" (IV.iv.27–28)—for it is
a pastime that suggests the argumentativeness of Rome enve-
loped in the clouds of incense that form part of the celebration of
the mass. Again, following this line of argument, Wasp maintains
that he would never try to pass himself off as an Anglican minister by pleading benefit of clergy: "I scorn to be saved by my book,
i'faith I'll hang first:" (I.iv.6–7) this tutor would not claim that by
reading a Latin verse he could function as a Church of England
minister and so escape the death penalty.

III

That all three authority figures—Overdo, Busy, and Wasp—
are placed simultaneously in the stocks raises doubts about their
moral validity and reduces them all to a common footing. None is
superior. Indeed each can be regarded as misrepresenting a basic
value—law (Overdo), religion (Busy), and learning (Wasp)—or a
religious party—Established Church, Puritan, and Catholic—or
both. In terms of their success at dealing with life—and Bartholomew Fair is surely a good imitation of that—none has the advantage. In various disguises, Justice Adam Overdo wanders the
fair searching for "enormities," but he mistakes the innocent for
the guilty and confuses minor offenses with major crimes. In the
end, he acknowledges the wisdom that comes when Quarlous's
injunction "hath wrought upon my judgment, and prevailed."
For Quarlous gives Overdo sound advice respecting human falli-
bility and weakness: "You are but Adam, flesh and blood! You

have your frailty." In a similar vein, Rabbi Busy, for his part, finds the fair filled with "abominations."[17] But in his zealous attacks on the "merchandise of Babylon" for sale at the fair, Busy engages with the puppet Dionysus in a debate over the religious offensiveness of plays, a debate that is as contradictory as the game of vapours. Ultimately, Busy is "confuted" by the sexlessness of the puppet and, ironically, by the qualities they share:

> I'll prove, against e'er a Rabbin of 'em all, that my
> standing is as lawful as his; that I speak by
> inspiration as well as he; that I have as little to do
> with learning as he; and do scorn her helps as much as he.
> (V.v.97–100)

In the end, Busy, too, admits defeat—"the cause hath failed me"—and with his last words he accepts conversion: "I am changed, and will become a beholder with you!"

The last of these representative figures, Wasp, finds himself shocked and appalled to discover that like Cokes, he, too, has been robbed: indeed, the robbery was effected so artfully that the marriage license Wasp guarded was stolen right out of the box he carried. There is now nothing to distinguish the martinet from his pupil. Humphrey Wasp is speechless, possibly for the first time in his life. But Adam Overdo, the most humane of the three, having learned his lesson, understands that Wasp's experience is now similar to his own and Busy's: all three have failed. As Overdo has come to realize, since failure is basic to the human condition, they must all exercise patience and forebearance toward themselves and others: "Nay, Humphrey, if I be patient, you must be so too." And it is at this point, in the closing minute of the play, that Jonson has Overdo recite a Horatian phrase as he invites Wasp and Busy home with him to dinner: "*ad correctionem, non ad destructionem; ad aedificandum, non ad diruendum*"— "for correction, not for destruction; for building, not ruining"—(V.vi.108–9). What is of special interest is that these are the words James himself had quoted in one of his published speeches, that *To The Lords And Commons Of The Parliament At White-Hall* of 21 March 1609/10.[18] The point is that James' justice of the peace, who is like James in so many ways, has now come to practice his monarch's more benevolent view of English law. In Overdo, Jonson was not presenting a parody of James.[19] Instead, the playwright seems to have been signaling for the king and the court the benefits of adopting a more tolerant policy in matters of religion. And indeed in the epilogue to the play addressed to James, Jonson stresses the seriousness of his intent: to "have used . . . well" "the scope of writers, and what store / Of leave is given them."

The suggestion that *Bartholomew Fair* is a play about the need for religious tolerance gives a rather new meaning to Jonson's choice of setting, for the fair celebrated on St. Bartholomew's day is a particularly appropriate date and place for Catholics, Anglicans, and Puritans to receive a lesson on the need for understanding and charity. Since nearly all the pleasures and dangers of life can be experienced at the fair, it obviously provided a testing ground for one's moral or spiritual values. But what is perhaps even more important, making it especially relevant to this interpretation, is the fact that in its history the St. Bartholomew's Day celebration involved all three of these branches of Christianity.[20] The fair was held in an open, flat area of some three acres just beyond the medieval walls of the city and near the Priory Church of St. Bartholomew the Great from which it took its name. This fairground at Smithfield was formerly the site of the burning of Catholic martyrs under Henry VIII and, a few years later, of Protestant martyrs under his daughter, Mary. It seems that St. Bartholomew, an apostle who had been flayed alive, had given his name to a continuing tradition of religious persecution. How fitting that the last person to be executed at Smithfield was named Bartholomew: one Bartholomew Legate, a radical separatist who was burned to death in 1611.[21] Clearly, religious persecution and punishments had been carried out recently enough at Smithfield to be in everyone's memory. In addition, for Jonson to choose to set the action of his play on 24 August, the feast day of St. Bartholomew, would surely remind his audience of two more practices: first, since the accession of Elizabeth it was the day established for burning Catholic relics and religious icons, in effect purifying places of worship of vestiges of the old religion. Second, and more importantly, since 1572 it was the day for commemorating the St. Bartholomew Massacre in France, when Catholics there massacred thousands of Huguenots. Among English Protestants it was considered the bloodiest day since Herod slaughtered the Innocents.[22]

These associations would surely offer members of the Church of England as well as English Catholics grounds for responding to the fair and its holiday celebration. But the fair itself would also provide the basis for a much more violent reaction from left-wing Protestants. At Smithfield, Rabbi Busy finds much to attack: among the things that appall him, two are particularly significant. The gingerbread sold at the fair, that is baked in the traditional shapes of saints, icons, or even storybook characters like Goldylocks, make Joan Trash's goods detestable to his mind. These objects are "the merchandise of Babylon," and "the peeping of popery upon the stalls." (He describes Goldylocks as a "purple strumpet . . . in her yellow gown and green sleeves.") In Busy's view the gingerbread-seller's booth is "a shop of relics," an "idolatrous grove of images." (III.vi.84–90)

Casting himself as one of those saints martyred for his faith, Busy violently attacks the baked goods, boldly welcomes his arrest, and absurdly faces his punishment in the stocks, mocked for his false heroism. In a similar manner Busy later in the play tries to stop one of the puppet shows customarily performed at the fair. Here, too, as we have seen, he finds himself in a losing battle, outdebated by the handpuppet Dionysus, the god not only of wine and celebration but also of the theater. The fair, then, offers Jonson both a title and a symbol. As the setting for bringing together his three opposing religious groups, it serves to remind his audience of the sad history of persecution and intolerance that each has practiced, and, what is even more to the point, it suggests the absurdity and futility of their past behavior.

IV

Once at the fair, much of the action of the play revolves in and around the booth where roast pig is sold—one of the traditional delicacies of this holiday.[23] Through its extended range of activities, Ursula's roast pig booth provides a home for nearly all the sins of the flesh—wrath (the quarreling that makes up the game of "vapours"); gluttony (pig, bottled ale, and tobacco); greed (as a front for fencing stolen property); and especially the physical (the back room functioning as a bawdy house). Indeed, Ursula herself, gross and sweaty, is summed up by Rabbi Busy as one who "is above all to be avoided, having the marks upon her of the three enemies of man: the world, as being in the Fair; the devil, as being in the fire; and the flesh, as being herself." (III.vi.33–35) When she enters into the quarreling, Ursula first appears brandishing a firebrand; later in the scene (II.v.) she burns her leg with a scalding pan. By this means, as Jackson Cope has pointed out, Jonson transforms the pig woman into the figure of *Ate* or *Discordia*—"the very champion of discord, of the lust, theft, fighting, and litigation which dominate a legalistic world gone beserk"—for in this form she was depicted in the emblem books of Cesare Ripa and Vicenzo Cartari, "holding high a firebrand, goading on the quarrels, scalding her own *'gambe torte.'*" Jonson was, in fact, well acquainted with the imagery of such iconographical studies since he had turned to them as sources for the designs of his court masques.[24] After studying Ursula and the events at the fair, Cope concludes that what we are to learn from the play is "that law, strict justice, is more and less than flesh and blood can either abide or profit from."[25]

Yet the theme of "strict justice" is not of sufficient dramatic weight to give coherence to so sprawling a work.[26] Actually, as Leo Salingar has written, this deficiency is also true of most of the other theses put forth as the central argument of the play:

> It has been maintained that the governing idea of the play is the ridicule of false authority, or else the lapse of authority in social life, or else (with the court performance in mind) that the very 'absence' of order within the play is meant to point toward an ideal order embodied in the audience, James and his court. But the court, *ex hypothesi*, were absent from the Hope; and, while it is clear that pretensions to authority form an important component theme, they do not account ... for the meanders of the plot. Nor does Jonson suggest what established authority, legal, religious, or scholastic, could or should do to correct the follies on display.[27]

Moreover, as a comedy it is unusually easygoing, maintaining "a prevailing mood of benevolence and acceptance that represents a departure for Jonson from the more bitterly satiric spirit of most of his earlier productions."[28] This tone of geniality, rather uncharacteristic of earlier Jonson drama, is in keeping with what we are arguing is a central concern of the play: the importance of tolerance, of practicing a live-and-let-live attitude among Christians, whatever church they belonged to.

Through still another sequence of events in the plot and another group of characters Jonson again makes the point that no particular Christian church or sect can claim superiority. In this case the incidents involving the figure of Grace Wellborn serve as an additional means of stressing the theme of the equality of religious beliefs. Although Grace seems to have no identifiable religious affiliation, her name suggests that she represents a quality that all are in need of; as Anne Barton has observed, Jonson was dedicated "to the idea of the revelatory name."[29] Independent spirited and intelligent, Grace is "the only sensible peacemaker at the Fair."[30] Yet she remains beyond anyone's ultimate dominance or control. Adam Overdo has become her legal guardian, having purchased from the Crown the right to act in this capacity since she was a royal ward. As her guardian, Overdo has arranged her marriage to his brother-in-law Cokes, since this would keep her valuable estates in the Overdo-Cokes family.[31] Should she refuse, Grace would be subject to a steep penalty—the "value o'my land." (III.v.254)[32] But, as it turns out, Grace is amazingly rescued from so unfortunate a wedding. Quarlous and Winwife, two gentlemen in search of wealthy wives, manage to get the marriage license stolen so that Cokes's name can be replaced by that of another. And since Quarlous and Winwife are rivals for her hand, Grace decides to have "the next person that comes this way (because destiny has a high hand in business of this nature)" (IV.iii.47–48) choose which of the two young men she will marry.

Since that faith that can secure grace for its adherents would surely have a validity greater than any other, Jonson has organized the action of *Bartholomew Fair* in such a way that Grace, a sometime ward of the king's in the keeping of Overdo, escapes the control of any recognizable religious belief. She is rightly anxious to avoid a liaison with Cokes, admitting early in the play that she would marry "anybody else, so I might 'scape." (I.v.80–81) By leaving the choice of a husband to "the next person that comes this way," Grace enables Providence to become manifest in the appearance of the madman, Trouble-all. For his part, Trouble-all has about him something approaching the divine intervention embodied in one possessed by a kind of divine madness; he even acts with what seems to be heavenly inspiration. This disturbed individual was "put out on his place by Justice Overdo . . . and's run mad upon't. So that ever since, he will do nothing but by Justice Overdo's warrant; he will not eat a crust, nor drink a little, nor make him in his apparel ready. His wife, sir-reverence, cannot get him make his water or shift his shirt without his warrant." (IV.i.49–55) Fixated and compulsive in his insanity, Trouble-all is someone whose actions are governed by a mad devotion to what he takes to be the law. Grace's fate, then, seems to be determined not so much by what Leo Salingar calls "a zany *persona ex machina*" but rather by one whom Jackson Cope rightly labels "destiny's agent."[33] Grace herself logically reasons that she cannot choose between Quarlous and Winwife, for she knows them so slightly; since they "are both equal and alike," she will have the name of the man she will marry chosen arbitrarily by the next passerby. And the "high hand" of Providence makes Trouble-all appear at exactly the moment he is needed; as Quarlous realizes, "here's a fine ragged prophet, dropped down i'the nick!" So Trouble-all chooses Grace a husband, the appropriately named Winwife, freeing her from the exclusive guardianship of Overdo as well as from the intended marriage to Cokes. Though Winwife seems to be little more than his name, nothing more is needed. And Trouble-all, in his dementia, chooses Winwife as the more desirable suitor: "I do like him there, that has the best warrant. Mistress, to save your longing (and multiply him), it may be this." (IV.iii.87–88) For her part, Grace answers to a higher authority of unclear religious affiliation, and she identifies with no particular faith.

Trouble-all's role as divine agent does not end with selecting a husband for Grace. In fact, like a true *deus ex machina*, Trouble-all directly or indirectly provides the means to effect the play's resolution. By distracting the watch, he enables Overdo and Busy to escape from the stocks. By arousing Overdo's pity for his misfortune, Trouble-all teaches him the need to put into practice a more sympathetic administration of the rule of law; Overdo promises, "I will be more tender hereafter. I see compassion may become a justice." (IV.i.74–75) And when Overdo, in an effort to make amends, hands Quarlous, who is disguised as Trouble-all, a signed blank warrant, Quarlous is able to charge Winwife a commission for his marriage to Grace, marry the rich widow Dame Purecraft, and dictate the terms of the happy ending.

V

Though his play is not an allegory in which everyone embodies an abstract idea and every action masks a principle, nevertheless as we have seen, Jonson does establish particular religious associations for a few characters. And the three who serve as representatives of particular religious positions experience similar fates, finding themselves confined to the stocks, acknowledging their failure, and promising reform. Each has been guilty of persecuting the others, yet none has a special claim to grace. As Ian Donaldson has suggested, with Wasp's realization that "He that will correct another, must want fault in himself," (V.iv.99) "we are at the heart of the comedy; the farcical, festive reversals are allowed to carry profounder, Christian implications."[34]

By questioning various claims to religious authority, Jonson makes the case for equality among them.[35] This is surely not the only theme of the play, and, in fact, it is an aspect of the geniality of the work that might well escape an inattentive audience. But since, after all, the stage could prove a troublesome place to touch on matters of religion, this point must be inferred and treated as an aspect of a larger and more diffuse subject. The liberal position Jonson is advocating—whether from disillusionment with all religions or from his belief in the need for a greater common understanding among his countrymen—would be expressed indirectly through information left open to ambiguous and subtle interpretation.

In the performance at court, where Jonson could be sure he would be fully understood, he prepared in his defense a special prologue and epilogue acknowledging that ultimately the king's judgment alone determined what was acceptable. The opening greeting, "Your Majesty is welcome to a Fair," announces that the evening is given over to the hope of delighting him. Intending to put him in a favorable humor, Jonson reveals that James could expect to find a satiric treatment of the Puritans he despised so intensely, whose "petulant ways / Yourself have known, and have been vexed with long." They are an appropriate target in this play, after all, because of their intolerance.

Once the play is over, Jonson respectfully addresses the issue of what playwrights can be permitted—"Your Majesty hath seen the play, and you / Can best allow it"—since, after all, the playwright here has surely come close to challenging the limit. Rather than concern himself with the criticism of any lesser courtier, Jonson readily defers to those restrictions set in place by a king who best knows "the scope of writers, and what store / Of leave is given them, if they take not more, / And turn it into licence" so that they fall "to rage or licence break." Jonson is using the word "licence" as a pun: first he says that playwrights should not abuse their freedom ("turn it into licence"); then he says that they must not exceed ("break") the authorization ("licence") that defines their limits: in effect, "license" can suggest excess, restriction, and authorization. In the epilogue Jonson admits his boldness, appeals for the king's good will, and concludes by acknowledging royal supremacy in matters of literary judgment as well as government. This time, for all we know, Jonson could "happy be t'have pleased the king."

6

Perkin Warbeck and the Politics of 1632

More than a century after it was first written and acted, John Ford's *Perkin Warbeck* was revived in London on 19 December 1745. The play was plucked from obscurity, dusted off, and performed presumably because it had contemporary relevance: the story of the dissension caused by a pretender to the English throne was of particular interest at a time when Bonnie Prince Charlie was rousing his supporters. Interestingly enough, the players at Goodman's Fields theater were, it seems, merely replicating in their way what Ford and the Queen's Men had done at the Phoenix when the play was first acted in the 1630s. In both cases, the acting companies realized they could evade government censorship and comment on contemporary politics by staging a play that claimed to enact a much earlier historical event.

Indeed, if one considers the selection and manner in which events are dramatized by Ford in *Perkin Warbeck*—the careful altering of his source material—as well as the invention of personalities that have no basis in his historical documents, one is led to conclude that the playwright had in mind a specific contemporary reading for the story, one that would comment on matters involving both religion and politics in far more subtle ways than either Heywood or Rowley in their versions of chronicle history drama. Here the touch is far more delicate: by slight adjustments, alterations, and inventions Ford turns the Warbeck tale, which occurred at the end of the fifteenth century, into a close analogue of the situation in the England of the 1630s, involving Frederick, the elector Palatine, and his wife, Elizabeth, the daughter of James I and the embodiment of the Protestant cause in Europe. To make clear the parallel between current Stuart politics and the Warbeck story, we shall point out the connections between life and art that can be demonstrated by reviewing events in England at the time *Perkin Warbeck* was first staged.

During James's entire reign, one of the few decisions that met with the unqualified approval of his Protestant subjects was his choice of a bridegroom for his seventeen-year-old daughter, Elizabeth. Although the heirs of Savoy and Spain as well as the king of Sweden were potential suitors, James, in 1612, agreed that she should marry the Elector Frederick V, the Calvinist ruler of the Palatinate, the same age as Elizabeth and a popular favorite. The Palatinate made up in importance what it lacked in size, for its ruler acted both as the chief among the seven electors who chose the emperor for the imperial throne and as the Calvinist head of the Union of German Protestant Princes. The elector Palatine might even rise to higher positions: like his ancestor Rupert III who became emperor, Frederick himself might well gain additional titles. Indeed, the Spanish ambassador Alonso de Velasco reported that James "denied the suggestion that Frederick was an inferior alliance . . . , saying 'he doubted not but that his son-in-law would have the title of King within a few years.' When the ambassador enquired further, he learned that the statement was made 'in respect of the crown of Bohemia because they pretend it to be elective.' "[1]

The difference of opinion alluded to in these remarks over the naming of a successor to the Bohemian crown soon became a crucial matter. Did the prerogative belong to the Habsburgs, the current rulers, who considered Bohemia their possession and intended it to remain in their hands, or was the monarch of Bohemia constitutionally elected, as some Protestants in particular believed? Moreover, the anti-Catholic legacy of Jerome of Prague and John Hus, burned for heresy in 1417, had left Bohemia more Protestant than Catholic and acutely sensitive to matters touching on political and religious life.

Although the Bohemian estates agreed in 1617 to continued Habsburg rule, the infringement on Protestant rights to worship carried out by the emperor Matthias's deputies prompted the revolt of May 1618 and the famous Defenestration of Prague. The rebels set up a provisional government and ordered an army to be raised, but it quickly became apparent that if the rejection of

Habsburg authority was to be permanent, the Bohemian nobles would have to enlist outside support. The best way in which to do this was by withdrawing their allegiance to Matthias's successor, Archduke Ferdinand, and offering the crown to a leading Protestant prince. The obvious choice was the Elector Frederick, and on 26 August 1619 the Bohemian estates elected him as their king. On the last day of October Frederick and Elizabeth made their triumphant entry into Prague as king and queen of Bohemia.

These were troubling events for the major European power blocks—the Habsburg dynasty, Britain, the United Provinces, France, Denmark, Sweden, and even the principality of Transylvania and the dukedom of Savoy. Ultimately, they were all drawn into a conflict named, after its duration, the Thirty Years' War. But in 1619, the news that Protestants had accepted the throne of Bohemia was greeted joyously in England, bonfires and bells marked the celebrating in London, and volunteers rushed to sign up in support of Frederick and Elizabeth. To English Protestants, John Hus was a stirring and memorable example of religious martyrdom—his story was vividly recounted with illustrations in Foxe's omnipresent and influential *Book of Martyrs*—and now Protestant dominance was being established at last in his country. Moreover, Elizabeth was, after her brother, the successor to the Stuart throne, and her five-year-old son, Prince Frederick Henry, was in 1619 the heir-presumptive to England as well as the Palatine and Bohemia.

But King James was more troubled than pleased. Unsure of the legality of the election and worried over its consequences, James was reluctant to call his son-in-law the "King of Bohemia," yet Frederick "let it be freely understood that he will not treat with the French ambassadors or with others unless they give him the title of king." Although Sir Horace Vere, who was allowed to muster a small English expeditionary force, was "given leave and orders to call him the most powerful and renowed King of Bohemia," James's own ambassadors

> have obtained some liberty of action in this matter . . . and they propose a compromise to call him the King elect of Bohemia, the word elect saving all respects. His Majesty, however, in writing to his son-in-law, gives him no title but "my son," in French.[2]

James's irresolution was evident as early as 1620: "the king, unwilling to call a Parliament, sits still, seeing what will be done without him; he even refused to second the King of Bohemia's request to the City of London for a loan of 100,000 pounds; he will not engage in any way till the arrival of Gondomar [the Spanish ambassador]."[3]

The King of England was distressed on several counts. Could he continue the negotiations with Spain, renewed in 1617, over a possible marriage of the infanta with Prince Charles? Could he support his daughter and son-in-law without also approving of a dangerous precedent—a subject's right to rebel against a monarch, as the Bohemians had done against archduke Ferdinand? Could he endanger English neutralism, abandon his policy of peace, and throw aside his role as peacemaker by involving his country in a costly religious war on the Continent? Could he actually persuade Parliament to raise sufficient funds to defend Frederick's claim to Bohemia in an effective way, should he decide to aid his son-in-law? Naturally, the more militaristic Protestants thought this the opportunity to defend and strengthen their coreligionists in Europe and oppose Spanish ambitions in the Low Countries. Even those less militaristic thought that family ties would ultimately make it impossible for James to remain uninvolved. But both were wrong. Apart from some token (and inexpensive) efforts on their behalf, James refused to commit himself to military action to support Frederick and Elizabeth. And he held to this course even as their cause became desperate, even when they were forced after great hardship to seek refuge in the Hague. The defeat of the unaided Frederick at the Battle of the White Mountain roused such public anger in England that in December 1620 James issued a proclamation against "Lavish and Licentious Speech of matters of State," i.e., criticism of his policies:

> there is at this time a more licentious passage of lavish discourse, and bold Censure in matters of State then hath been heretofore, or is fit to be suffered, Wee have thought it necessary . . . to command them and every of them, from the highest to the lowest, to take heede, how they intermeddle by Penne, or Speech, with causes of State, and secrets of Empire, either at home, or abroad . . . .[4]

The intensity of his Protestant subjects' dislike of their king's policy is easy to understand. James's failure to come to Elizabeth's aid shocked many, whose dismay was compounded by the king's lengthy, ongoing discussions with Spain for a marriage of the prince of Wales with the infanta. When this effort ended in 1623 with the return from Madrid of Prince Charles and the duke of Buckingham, bonfires and bells now celebrated a wedding that would not take place.

Indeed, for militant Protestants in England, Elizabeth of Bohemia, undeterred and indefatigable even in exile, was seen as the figurehead of their cause. With her husband cast as a kind of resurrected Prince Henry, Elizabeth, youthful, lively, and fair, was thought of as a new Queen Elizabeth. Sir Thomas Roe, serving in James's diplomatic service, wrote to Elizabeth: "I may assure your Majesty a joyful truth, I never shall see any so beloved here that dwells not here, nor any cause so affected as yours."[5] But the young couple could not leave Europe: their popularity in England was so great that James forbade them to seek refuge in his own kingdom. Evidently, Elizabeth's father feared that public opinion might even "provoke an uprising which would overturn the succession in their favour."[6]

The terms of mockery invented by Catholic opponents as labels for Elizabeth and Frederick became titles of distinction and sympathy in the language of their Protestant supporters. For example, having reigned in Bohemia for only one winter before being driven out, the elector and his wife were ridiculed as "the Winter King and Queen" by their enemies, but for Protestants, naturally, this name was used with melancholy sympathy. To his enemies Frederick was also derisively known as " 'faithless Fritz' or the King of Hearts, the most worthless King of the pack," but this sobriquet was transformed into a compliment, especially for Elizabeth, who was adoringly praised as "the Queen of Hearts."[7]

Her brother, while Prince of Wales, was enthusiastic in support of Elizabeth and Frederick, even angering the ailing and exhausted king by his energetic proposals on their behalf. And Charles was constant in his feelings even after he ascended the throne and married his French Catholic princess. But ironically, although he had urged his father to take more forceful action and although he had intended to become more active on their behalf when he could, circumstances were to deny him the opportunity. Once crowned, Charles could not find a way of governing effectively with Parliament, and without it, he could not finance any undertaking to restore what had been lost in the Palatine. As Carola Oman observes:

> The tale had always been that King James possessed the means but not the will to take action on behalf of the King of Bohemia. It was now obvious that King Charles possessed the will but not the means.[8]

But in the eyes of many English Protestants the importance of Elizabeth and Frederick was undiminished. Even when Charles and Henrietta Maria had their first son in 1630,

> there were those in England who did not share the general joy; they muttered that there were Protestant heirs enough to the crown, in the flourishing offspring of the Queen of Bohemia; and that they needed none from the Popish stock of their French Queen.[9]

Elizabeth's popularity among the English never waned: the so-called *corantos*, the Protestant-biased newspapers of the day, reported the latest events from the Continent; Elizabeth's own indefatigable correspondence with her English friends such as Lucy, the countess of Bedford, kept the queen of Bohemia's story current; and her supporters were unfailing in their efforts.[10] Although the power and position of the Puritan coalition at court was declining in the 1620s, Elizabeth provided a focus for their concern: the third earl of Pembroke, acting as her counselor on political matters, was moved to joy or sorrow above all by the way affairs affected the prospects of the king and queen of Bohemia; and among others, the third earl of Southampton even tried to raise a volunteer force to go to their aid.[11]

Given her stature as a symbol of the Protestant cause, Elizabeth became a figure of enormous public sympathy when the English learned of Frederick's unexpected death of the plague in 1632 at the age of thirty-six.

> The Queen of Bohemia's devotion to her husband was so well known that the news of his death reached England with melodramatic additions. In the streets of London citizens learnt without sur-

prise that the Lady Elizabeth had been unable to survive her mate. For over a week even the inhabitants of Whitehall believed this sequel probable. Mr. William Boswell, British envoy at the Hague, sent word that those closest about the queen much doubted whether she would long be able to bear her grief.[12]

Suddenly, after nineteen years of very happy marriage, she was a widow living in exile, in difficult circumstances, with twelve children whose futures were most insecure. How could any committed Protestant playwright not think of her and her unhappy plight?

Actually the unhappy situation of the elector and his wife had already been dramatized several times and in different genres. Thomas Drue's *The Life of the Duchess of Suffolk* (1624) derives its plot from Foxe's *Book of Martyrs* but alters its source material to reflect incidents involving Elizabeth of Bohemia;[13] Dekker and Ford's *The Sun's Darling* (March 1623/24) is "a militant Protestant or apocalytic masque" in support of the Winter King and Queen;[14] and Philip Massinger's *Believe As You List* (1631), though set in Carthage, alludes to King Sebastian of Portugal, "an exile and a supplicant for aid in Europe in the 1580's," whose situation was analogous to that of Frederick and Elizabeth, "equally a tragedy of betrayal."[15]

Ford, a staunch Protestant playwright, evidently felt drawn to call audience attention to the lamentable fate of the popular queen of Bohemia. His collaboration with Dekker on *The Sun's Darling* as well as on several other plays suggests that the two men shared not only artistic but also political convictions. As Julia Gasper has shown, Dekker is among the most forceful of Protestant writers. His commitment to the Reformation, to a united Reformed church (combining Lutherans and Calvinists), to international alliances with Protestant powers, and to the defense of Protestants under Catholic attack exceeded that of his fellow playwrights and held sway even when he collaborated with them. Indeed, Dekker's belief in the need for military intervention against Rome

> was stronger and more lasting than any other writer's, and he was the author of *The Whore of Babylon*, which can be called the definitive

militant Protestant play. When in his later career Dekker collaborated with younger writers such as Massinger and Ford, the results
are still consistent with his own previous work.[16]

Judging Ford's politics by the company he kept, we can place the
author of *Perkin Warbeck* among those sympathetic to the Protestant causes Dekker so earnestly supported.

Moreover, such a work as *The Chronicle Historie of Perkin
Warbeck* could offer its creator protection, under the guise that it
merely dramatizes historical fact, even while it presents criticism
with immediate, contemporary social or political relevance.
Playgoers are quick to interpret staged instances according to
contemporary examples; and by the application of a little ingenu-
ity and a lot of analogy, a text that per se has no current political,
social, or religious relevance can be transformed in performance
into a topical work of social protest. With this in mind, we should
consider the possible implications of Ford's unique effort in this
genre—an effort that the playwright himself acknowledges in the
prologue as "out of fashion," especially if his was not the first
play to be written on Perkin Warbeck's claim to the throne of
England.[17]

Actually, the historical events lend themselves to dramatic
presentation, for they pit two neighboring rival kings—Henry
VII and James IV—against each other and place Warbeck, an
imposter, as a pawn of the defeated Yorkists and of the Scots.
But, ignoring history, Ford turns Warbeck into a puzzling and
sympathetic figure: his hero truly thinks himself the rightful king
of England, and, moreover, he acts with greater dignity and
forthrightness than either his supporters or his enemies.[18] In
T. S. Eliot's opinion, Ford "succeeded in a most difficult attempt;
and the play of *Perkin Warbeck* is almost flawless."[19]

We can determine the date of the writing and acting of *Perkin
Warbeck*, essential for placing it in its contemporary context, with
some precision. Ford's principal sources were Bacon's *History of
the Reign of King Henry VII* (1622) and Thomas Gainsford's *The
True and Wonderfull History of Perkin Warbeck* (1618). But the
play was first entered in the Stationers' Register in February
1634 as it was "Acted (some-times) by the Queenes Majesties

Servants at the Phoenix in Drurie Lane."[20] The "some-times" is an unusual adjective in this description, probably signifying "formerly," i.e. shortly before the 1634 printing. *Perkin Warbeck*, then, was probably completed in 1632/33. The establishment of this as the date of final composition is important since it coincides with the death of Frederick in 1632.[21]

Two other extratextual facts suggest that Ford's work had political implications. First, Sir Henry Herbert, the master of the revels, while approving *Perkin Warbeck* for performance made a cautionary note on the manuscript which was recorded in the Stationers' Register entry: "observing the Caution in the License." Exactly why "Caution" was especially necessary is unexplained; a play about a hero who challenges the legitimacy of an English king might be unsettling enough to deserve a warning, but it is also possible that the play came disconcertingly close to particular recent events, and that Herbert attempted to provide himself with some cover.

A second fact that suggests a political subtext is Ford's dedication of the play to William Cavendish, the earl of Newcastle. In 1633/34 Cavendish was a busy patron of the arts, commissioning Ben Jonson to devise entertainments for Charles at both Welbeck and Bolsover. These efforts were an unsuccessful attempt to acquire greater influence over the king's politics. Cavendish, according to Martin Butler,

> was no puritan but neither was he a simple courtier for, by birth . . . and temperament an Elizabethan, he was out of his depth in Charles's progressive court, isolated, distrustful and saddened by the decline of the English nobility. In 1632 he declared himself a lord of misrule, for 'I take that for an honor in these dayes rather then the other more common title.'[22]

Since Cavendish's views were "patriotic, nostalgic for England's Elizabethan greatess . . . [and] discontent with a Frenchified, unheroic court and its king," he distanced himself from the policies of the court party.[23] Ford's dedication of the play suggests that Cavendish approved of it.[24]

The date of the work, the "Caution in the license," and the dedication all suggest that Ford may well have had something more than a straightforward chronicle play in mind when he turned to the story of Perkin Warbeck. Indeed, in some ways it and Massinger's *Believe As You List* are typical of the kind of love histories written under the Stuarts. Anne Barton has observed how in both plays

> an amoral and unglamorous monarch [such as Henry VII] . . . is used to set off a king figure of another and more nostalgic kind [such as Perkin]. . . . The individual who looks and speaks like a monarch is, in some sense, a pretender: a claimant whose actual title to the throne, whatever the emotions aroused by his personality, is fictional, or impossible to prove.[25]

Philip Edwards, too, speculates that these plays treat discredited pretenders with dignity in order to present them as heroes, as

> luminous figure[s] appearing from the mists announcing that . . . the dead past [is] newly come alive in order to bring succour to an ailing nation. . . . A charismatic figure of lost royalty would have had a great emotional appeal at a period when many of Charles's subjects looked on the occupant of the throne as the dried husk of a king.[26]

All of these associations suggest that Ford's play, as its title states, may truly be as much "a strange truth" as a "chronicle historie." Perhaps the best way to identify this "strange truth"— the contemporary political subtext for the story of Perkin Warbeck—will be to compare Ford's sources with his dramatization of them. In this way we can isolate aspects of the work that were shaped entirely by the dramatist and consider to what degree these elements were invented because they reflected contemporary circumstances or aroused audience response toward them.

Surely the most notable and fascinating aspect of Ford's play involves his creation of the characters of Perkin Warbeck and his bride, the Scottish princess Katherine Gordon. To turn first to the title character, Ford's hero is unique in that he never wavers in his conviction that he is in reality Richard Duke of York, the younger son of Edward IV and therefore the rightful ruler of England. He is never subject to doubt or hesitancy. And unlike the historical Warbeck, this hero never confesses that he is an imposter. What Ford presents instead is a purely invented figure, impressive in language and appearance, certain of his royal origins.[27] Moreover, this unwavering hero, despite the crew around him, seems ultimately admirable in pursuit of his claim to the throne. As a consequence the action of the play suggests that other pretenders may also be well persuaded of their right to rule and may well make attractive rulers. Naturally, another "pretender," the Elector Prince Frederick V who had been crowned king of Bohemia, was the contemporary whose problems most closely matched those of the hero in *Perkin Warbeck*.[28] And rather like Perkin, who, though a captive, "still a'will be king" (V.iii.156), so Frederick in defeat, when asked by his Catholic opponents to offer a formal submission and apology, "replied, with inspired simplicity, that a man who was in the right could not apologize. . . . To the end of his life he still declared that he . . . was the rightful King of Bohemia, unlawfully attacked both there and in his German lands."[29]

In their personalities the fictional hero of Ford's play and the historical figure of the elector Palatine also share similarities. Basing his reading on Gainsford's account, Ford characterizes Warbeck as "effeminently dolent" when he criticizes the Scottish king for the brutality of his attacks across the border into England (III.iii.56–76). Tenderhearted and ineffectual, Warbeck, despite his plans and activities, his self-image and his oratory, accomplishes very little on the battlefield. The same could be said of Frederick. Sir Dudley Carleton, English ambassador to the States-General, remarked that Frederick, once settled in exile in the Hague, seemed "more liable to run away than to fight."[30] Indeed, as early as 1622 "a hostile observer . . . questioned the wisdom of electing 'a man who had never seen either a battle or a corpse, . . . a prince who knew more about gardening than fighting.' "[31] C. V. Wedgwood notes that Frederick "was strong neither in body nor in spirit, and the gentle education which had been planned to stimulate his timorous nature and to fit him for the arduous championship of a cause had softened out of existence what little character he had."[32] This truth was no secret to the English. As the prince of Wales realized, in the marriage of Frederick and his sister, the elector Palatinate acted as a figurehead, but it was Elizabeth's energy and wit that served as the driving force: Charles wrote, "The grey mare is the best horse."[33]

Ford is even more inventive in reworking his sources to create the character of Perkin's wife. The playwright turns a rather shadowy figure in the histories into one of the major characters of his play, greatly expanding her importance in the story. She appears in as many scenes as Warbeck, and she has almost half as many lines as he does. Peter Ure, who calls her character "virtually flawless in the coherence of its imagining," points out that she

> has no counterpart in the sources. In seeking an origin for her, we are reduced to those rather unsatisfactory suppositions about 'germs' and 'hints' that are used to beg so many questions in Shakespearean source-study. It can be placed on record that in Bacon there is a sentence, in Gainsford a few pages, and in *Albion's England* the crudest of adumbrations—of all three we can say that at the least they would not have proved inimical to Ford's invention of Katherine and that at the most they would have given him some slight warrant . . . for what he did.[34]

Indeed, the qualities Ford gives Katherine Gordon strengthen the similarities between her imagined life and fortunes and those of Elizabeth of Bohemia. Like Elizabeth of Bohemia, Katherine is "a princess of the royal blood of Scotland." (I.ii.l.104) According to Bacon, she is "a near kinswoman to the King himself, and a young virgin of excellent beauty and virtue."[35] Also like Elizabeth, Katherine's choice of husband is determined by the king. (In the sources James IV agrees to but does not initiate the marriage.) In fact, the scene in which King James gives Katherine to Warbeck (II.iii) is original with Ford, who rejects the euphuistic account of Warbeck's wooing of Katherine found in Gainsford's history.[36]

The importance of her own independent character, as Ford has drawn her, is not to be underestimated. Her devotion to Perkin serves to enhance him; the implication is that if she finds him so worthy, we should, too, for in her own person Katherine is most impressive, "a pattern / For every virtuous wife." (V.iii.93–94)[37] Ford has altered his sources always with the effect of making her an exceptionally appealing and sympathetic figure. For example, he knew but makes no mention of the fact that the historical Katherine remarried three times; his Katherine, in a manner that suggests Elizabeth's devotion to Frederick, emphasizes both her desire to remain with Warbeck and her undying love for him: "I swear / To die a faithful widow to thy bed." (V.iii.151–52) She insists on sharing his fortune though they know that "princes cast out of their thrones" teach one what Elizabeth and Frederick were learning: that "misery / Is destitute of friends or of relief." (III.iv.78–80) Moreover, by organizing his material so that Katherine appears in every scene in the last act, Ford can stress the deprivation she suffers from the loss of family, husband, and throne. And like Elizabeth, she will not return to her homeland:

> As for my native country, since it once
> Saw me a princess in the height of greatness
> My birth allowed me, here I make a vow
> Scotland shall never see me being fallen
> Or lessened in my fortunes. Never, Jane,
> Never to Scotland more will I return.
> (V.i.19–24)

Her last act is the parting kiss she requests from her condemned husband, who will not deny his claim to the throne to save his life. Fainting with grief and sorrow, yet raised to an even greater dignity by the reconfirmation of their love, Katherine is pathetically helped off stage by her faithful suitor Dalyell and her lady in waiting.[38] This last image of her can hardly fail to find a sympathetic response from an audience—exactly what a supporter of Elizabeth of Bohemia would hope for.

Finally, to suggest without doubt that his characters should bring to mind contemporary equivalences, Ford twice refers to the popular nicknames for Frederick and Elizabeth: one of Perkin's supporters cries, "Save thee, king of hearts!" (IV.v.32), and earlier Perkin tells his bride [your] "heart . . . / Shall crown you queen of me." (II.iii.82–83)[39]

Ford has shaped not only some of his characters but also some of the speeches and incidents to suggest a contemporary parallel to his treatment of the story. His Henry VII is the successful king of England in part because he is a pragmatist, knowing that "Money gives soul to action:" without "the food of fit supplies" that money can provide, "courage, need, and want" can do little. Moreover, Henry works with his Parliament and insists on the full payment of subsidies they have approved: "We'll not abate

one penny what in parliament / Hath freely been contributed."
(III.i.27–28) His opponents come to appreciate this, too, for they
realize that his subsidies are the means that "Henry / Of England hath in open field o'erthrown / The armies who opposed
him." (III.iv.84–86) Victory in military engagements requires
both that Parliament approve subsidies and that the Crown in-
sist on their thorough collection. This insistence on the need for
king and Parliament to cooperate is significant. By contrast, neither James nor Charles could persuade Parliament to raise
funds sufficient to wage a successful war on behalf of Frederick
and the Protestant cause, and by 1634 Charles's "Non-Parlia-
mentary" or "Personal Rule" was five years old.

Parallels between the behavior of Frederick's father-in-law
and Warbeck's Scottish king are also stressed. As C. V. Wedgwood points out, King James was torn: on the one hand, he desired to play peacemaker and knew he could never sustain for
any length of time the cost of an army powerful enough to secure
Frederick's position; on the other hand, he would have liked to
aid his daughter and son-in-law, placate his Protestant subjects,
and prevent Catholic powers from dominating the United Provinces and controlling the Rhine. So "the King of England celebrated his son-in-law's accession by officially denying to every
sovereign in Europe that he had countenanced or even known
of the project [to accept the crown of Bohemia]," though at the
last possible moment James was persuaded to allow Sir Horace
Vere to sail for the Low Countries from Gravesend with a volunteer force of two thousand men.[40] In the eyes of those who followed court politics, James could only look inconsistent and self-
serving, not subtle and wise.

Inconsistent and self-serving behavior also characterizes
Ford's James IV. Early in the play the king of Scotland argues
that monarchs have the right to aid allies who have lost their
crowns, citing Richard Coeur-de-Lion and Robert Bruce as instances of those who: "Both sought, and found, supplies from
foreign kings / To repossess their own." (II.i.27–28) And as further support for Warbeck's claim, he notes that

> king Charles of France
> And Maximilian of Bohemia both
> Have ratified his [Warbeck's] credit by their letters.
>   (II.i.29–31)

But though at first the Scottish king takes up Warbeck's standard—"Thou never shalt repent that thou hast put / Thy cause and person into my protection" (106–7)—he ultimately yields to the astute, tempting diplomatic negotiations of Spain and England. Even though he is linked to Warbeck by marriage, James disclaims any obligation to him, behavior that would remind many in Ford's audience of the actions of their own King James, who had failed to fulfill his obligations, or at least the obligations implicit when he married his daughter to the elector Palatine.

In Ford's play agents from the rulers of Spain and England visit James to broker an agreement that will result in "a league / Of amity," joining Scotland and England with "France, Spain, and Germany." Among its advantages, this peace will secure trade with the Low Countries and the Habsburgs:

> The English merchants, sir, have been received
> With general procession into Antwerp;
> The emperor confirms the combination.
>
> (IV.iii.5–7)

And the way Ford's Scottish king can achieve this happy end could not be simpler: all he needs to do is abandon Warbeck. James can then expect to marry Princess Margaret, the sister of England's Henry VII, and look forward to a time of peace and prosperity:

> A league with Ferdinand, a marriage
> With English Margaret, a free release
> From restitution for the late affronts,
> Cessation from hostility! and all
> For Warbeck not delivered, but dismissed!
> We could not wish it better.
>
> (IV.iii.56–61)

Like the issues raised in the play, the conditions for and the advantages of a royal marriage preoccupied the English court for much of the 1620s—and the implied condition for Charles' match with the Spanish infanta was that James abandon his son-in-law Frederick.[41] Moreover, by mentioning even briefly so many of the countries, names, and places involved in the Thirty Years' War—Spain, France, Antwerp, Maximilian of Bohemia—Ford's drama manages to strengthen the similarities between its story and contemporary politics.

In *Perkin Warbeck*, Ford has provided a Protestant commentary on his own political world disguised as a chronicle history of the late fifteenth century. Little wonder that Sir Henry Herbert insisted on "observing the Caution in the License," for this play can be best understood by the analogy it draws between the characters and incidents of the play and those of recent history. Unlike James and Charles, Henry VII is a model for modern rulers, achieving stability for his crown through a combination of financial strength, cooperation with Parliament, and diplomacy—including both spies, informers, and secret emissaries. Like his Scots descendants, James IV appears weak and opportunistic because he cannot sustain the moral obligations he incurs. Like Frederick and Elizabeth, Perkin and Katherine, though defeated, are exemplary for their devotion and convictions. And at the conclusion of Ford's play, the audience is left with feelings of sympathy and admiration for a figure who is a surrogate for the recently widowed Elizabeth of Bohemia, a symbol of the true Protestant cause abandoned by the Stuarts, who have made a French Catholic the queen of England and named Archbishop Laud to institute what seem proto-Catholic practices and ceremonies.[42]

7

Conclusion: "Where truth is hid"

IN THE PLAYS DISCUSSED IN THE PRECEDING CHAPTERS, EACH playwright takes up issues involving the religious controversy of the age in ways that the Revels Office would find inoffensive, despite the prohibition against the theater dealing with matters of church and state. Marlowe uses ambiguity as his stalking horse in *Dr. Faustus*; Shakespeare employs a kind of ambivalence in *Measure for Measure*. For their part, Rowley in *When You See Me You Know Me* and Heywood in *If You Know Not Me You Know Nobody* privilege those orthodox views that present an implicit criticism of the actions taken by the Stuart court. And finally, in our last two examples, the encoded meaning is implied on the one hand through the inclusion of insignificant facts, as in the geography of place names in Jonson's *Bartholomew Fair*, or on the other hand through analogy, as in Ford's *Perkin Warbeck*, which alters its sources in order to create a deliberate resemblance between the characters and plot in the play and those recent events involving Frederick V, the elector Palatine, and Elizabeth Stuart, his wife.

By focusing on these six plays—identifying their particular way of communicating and placing them in their political context—we can appreciate how pervasively the drama was affected by matters of religion, until such matters closed down the theaters completely. For Renaissance audiences, questions of faith involved how eternity might be spent, and heaven and hell were too real and important to be out of one's thoughts for long. Since the government was in the continual process of establishing an official position on matters of doctrine and practice, the Revels Office was responsible for seeing that the official view, the bias of the moment, was not seriously threatened. Nevertheless, since most questions of faith cannot receive definitive answers in this life, doubts and alternatives were naturally being expressed. Over these intensely held and opposing beliefs, all competing for expression in the theater, the master of the revels, as we noted earlier, had the task of keeping some control. And, indeed, he seems with no little success to have managed to sail smoothly among the political sects and factions that from moment to moment directed the shifting winds of government policy on religious questions. A censorship was in place that could threaten but that rarely acted in a threatening way, and matters of faith found subtle and artistic voice on the Renaissance stage.

In our discussion of Marlowe's play, we pointed out how indeterminate are the causes of Faustus's longings. Marlowe has managed matters so that *Dr. Faustus* can be regarded in a straightforward way without emphasizing any of its intellectual or theological subtleties.[1] At the same time, especially for the more thoughtful, the play can also raise serious questions about a number of the tenets both in Calvinist theology and in the doctrines of the Church of England. Indeed, the plays that we have examined in this study served to raise just such doubts or support religious positions at odds with government policy. And by raising such questions and challenging government policy, the theater inevitably dramatized a range of possibilities beyond what was officially sanctioned. As Steven Mullaney has argued:

> In an age when the domain in which knowledge was produced and circulated was still a relatively contained system, any significant expansion of that domain . . . threatened to become a difference in kind as well—to . . . force a transition from a relatively limited and closed symbolic system to a more radically open economy of knowledge and representation.

That the theater, not quite legitimate or respectable, was functioning in such a way made its status even more uncertain.

> [T]he Elizabethan public theater emerged from and appropriated a place within the fissures and contradiction of the cultural landscape; although it rapidly became, in Jean Howard's words, 'one of the chief ideological apparatuses of Elizabethan society,' it was neither the product nor the organ of the state but rather the result of a historically determined collusion between artisanal enterpreneurs and a socially diverse and astoundingly large audience.[2]

To glimpse something of the ways that Renaissance audiences responded to the implications of the plays they saw requires us not only to make use of historical documentation—such as the remarks of Henry Harte or the words of Josias Nicholls on predestination quoted in chapter 2—but also to attempt an imaginative reconstruction of their theater experiences, traditions, and associations. We know that conventions affect expectations: since we will see what we expect to see, we know that theatergoers anticipate what previous experience has taught them to expect. Indeed, Shakespeare well understands this principle, for he deconstructs it in *Measure for Measure*. In this play conventional themes and characters familiar from earlier drama do not conform to traditional paradigms: the sadistic Angelo never undergoes a satisfactory penance and reformation; Mariana's love for him is presented as perverse and incomprehensible; Isabella remains silent before the marriage proposals of the Duke; and the Duke himself nearly fails in his obscure scheming while discovering an attraction to the opposite sex that comes as a surprise even to him.

And although *Measure for Measure* dramatizes the Calvinist belief in the "heavenly comforts of despair," the action and its resolution leave that matter problematic also. The play's lack of closure—Isabella's refusal to respond to the repeated proposals of the Duke—suggests that despair may not lead to such comforts after all, neither for her nor for anyone else. With its unresolved ending and with its characters who never measure up to the complete reformation found in their prototypes, Shakespeare seems determined that we will not leave a performance with our religious faith reassured, whatever the doctrines of that faith. The ambiguity of *Dr. Faustus* has been replaced by a kind of complex ambivalence in *Measure for Measure*.

By contrast, Rowley and Heywood's method originates neither in their devices of language nor in the subtlety or complexity with which they dramatize characters and ideas. Instead, they redefine a genre for their own purposes. Their quasi-historical entertainments are, in fact, works of religious propaganda. Using Foxe's *Book of Martyrs* as a primary source, *When You See Me You Know Me* and *If You Know Not Me You Know Nobody* demonstrate the power of the true faith and the importance to the continued well-being of the country of protecting the practices of

English Protestantism. These plays are the product of "Puritan or educated Protestant attempts to organise and enlist for their own purposes deep-rooted popular traditions."[3] Their constant reprintings—the two plays were reissued twelve times between 1605 and 1639—are an obvious Protestant response to the feelings of insecurity aroused by what could only be regarded as the blindness of the Stuarts to the dangers of international Catholicism. The instances are multiple: the siege and fall of Ostend (1601–4), the peace treaty with Spain (1604), the Gunpowder Plot (1605), the formation of the Catholic League (1609), the outbreak of war in Bohemia (1619), the negotiations for the Spanish match (1620–23), the deaths of Gustavus Adolphus and Frederick, the elector Palatine (1632), and the selection of Laud as archbishop of Canterbury (1633). Constantly restaged, these two plays were a continual reminder to their audiences that like the Israelites the English would live in a promised land under divine protection if only they remained the home of the true faith.

We will find nothing so apocalyptic in Ben Jonson's *Bartholomew Fair*. His truth is hinted through association: he implies meaning through his choice of the names of places and people— Harrow on the Hill, Banbury, Bartholomew Fair, Overdo, Grace. In this way, the playwright links his main characters to religious positions. Then by maneuvering his characters into situations that are mutually embarrassing, Jonson can show how they are all, as is the fashion with fallen humanity, liable to failure and in need of forgiveness. Ultimately, the happy ending can come about only through the acknowledgment of mutual recognition and respect. As Shakespeare's mechanicals might say, here is a play fitted, and one that has the temerity not only to evade the censor, but also, when performed before the court, to offer advice on religious matters to the king himself. Naturally, for this ploy to work, the audience must be aware of the associations of religious practices with geographical places—for example Catholics with Harrow on the Hill, Puritans with Banbury, and the persecution of both Catholics and Protestants with Bartholomew Fair—but one hardly thinks that the first audiences required instruction in such matters.

As our last example of "truth . . . hid indeed / Within the center," we traced the analogies worked out by John Ford between the history of Perkin Warbeck, the pretender to the throne of

Henry VII, and the plight in the early 1630s of Frederick, the elector Palatine, and his wife. Ford's religious sympathies can be identified by his association with Thomas Dekker, the most militant of the Protestant playwrights of the period. And the alterations and additions Ford made to his sources seem directed at arousing public support for the plight of the recently widowed Elizabeth and her twelve children, especially since this spirited and popular "Queen of Hearts," a devout Calvinist and the sister of the king of England, was the standard bearer of the Protestant cause in Europe.

Surely playwrights did not dramatize these stories simply because they made exciting stage works or displayed the puppets going through their old paces. Instead, the most successful dramatists managed to offer their audiences commentary on contemporary issues—even on the risky topic of religion—in ways that would not provoke the Revels Office but that an astute spectator would quickly grasp. The situation ultimately proved fortuitous: on the one hand, without the threat of censorship, serious drama might well have turned into straightforward propaganda; on the other hand, with censorship too greatly enforced, serious drama might have been strangled. By maintaining a balance between prohibitions that were too absolute or too lax, the theater remained a vital institution of contemporary life. Audiences could find in the playhouse both diversion and relevance. Expecting the action to touch on problems and issues common to all, intelligent theatergoers came prepared to interpret, to decode, to translate, and to analogize. For the perceptive, the pleasures of the afternoon could engage the mind as well as the heart.

Notes

CHAPTER 1. INTRODUCTION:
RELIGION AND STAGE CENSORSHIP

1. For a discussion of the play and the problems it presents see Howard-Hill, ed., *Shakespeare and Sir Thomas More* and McMillin, *Elizabethan Theatre*.

2. Chambers, *Elizabethan Stage*, 4:306.

3. Dollimore, *Radical Tragedy*, 23.

4. Greenblatt, *Shakespearean Negotiations* (Berkeley: University of California Press, 1988), 16. In the extensive and recent study, *Press Censorship*, Cyndia Susan Clegg comes to the conclusion that press control was "largely reactive rather than proactive even though its mechanisms were well defined." (31) "Elizabethan censorship proclamations, all particular measures directed toward particular texts, testify to the degree to which press censorship between 1558 and 1603 proceeded *ad hoc* rather than by unifying principle. . . . No single common denominator unifies all the proclamations except reliance on the due process of English law. . . . [With some exceptions] the principal end of censorship was suppressing religio-political texts—either Catholic writings that denied Elizabeth's supremacy and advocated placing a Catholic monarch on the English throne, or radical Protestant texts that denied the Queen's authority over religion. . . . The suppression of texts censored by proclamation was largely ineffective. . . . [But in their effect] they consolidated English nationalism and constructed a benevolent relationship between Elizabeth and her subjects, with censorship represented as a desperate resort taken to ensure this relationship." This was unlike the situation under James in which the censorship proclamations are divisive articulating "a genuinely oppositional stance between a Divine Right King and his subjects." (75–76).

5. Patterson, *Censorship and Interpretation*, 44–58.

6. In an intriguing article, "The Powerless Theater," Paul Yachnin argues that the theater was, in effect, "powerless and indeed irrelevant to the system of power" because of what Annable Patterson has called the "functional ambiguity" it practiced in order to evade the censors, because of its commercial requirement to be responsive to a public audience, and because of what was regarded as the separateness of poetry from the merely actual or factual. Yet, in Yachnin's view, these factors did not "preclude the theater's power to excite discussion concerning politics and social issues." ". . . Between 1590 and 1625, the stage persistently represented the issues of the moment but . . . these representations were seen to subsist in a field of discourse isolated from the real world . . . and seen normally as incapable of intervening in the political arena," 51.

7. Winwood, *Memorials of Affairs of State*, 2:64.

8. Collinson, *Elizabethan Puritan Movement*, 54.

9. Dutton, *Mastering the Revels*. I gratefully acknowledge the work of Dutton and the many others (cited in subsequent footnotes) whose recent publications on Renaissance stage censorship have enabled me to develop my argument.

10. Chambers, *Elizabethan Stage* 4:306.

11. Dutton, *Mastering the Revels*, 86, 89.

12. Ibid., 178.

13. Howard, "Renaissance Antitheatricality," 164.

14. Chambers, *Elizabethan Stage*, 4:306.

15. Burt, *Licensed by Authority*, 14.

16. Butler, "Ecclesiastical Censorship," 469. Butler is nicely restating the argument of Patterson in *Censorship and Interpretation*.

17. Sinfield, *Faultlines*, 113–14.

18. Joel B. Altman (*Tudor Play of Mind*) discusses how Renaissance students, trained to argue *in utramque partem*, on both sides of the question, naturally created a drama with "ambivalence and multiplicity of view" so that their plays "are essentially questions and not statements at all." (3–4, 6) In the case of *Doctor Faustus*, he concludes that the meaning "lies in the contrast between the hero's humanistic attempt to restore his freedom and his sadly diminished capacity for true freedom; in his ignorance of his own inadequacy; and, above all, in the discovery that hell is really the circumscribed consciousness." (388)

19. Schleiner, "Providential Improvisation," 227.

20. Patterson, *Censorship and Interpretation*, 44.

21. Greenblatt, "General Introduction," 38.

Chapter 2. *Dr. Faustus* and the Religious Controversy

1. Cole, *Suffering and Evil*, 231–32.

2. For a full discussion of the evolution of the morality play see Spivack, *Shakespeare and the Allegory of Evil*.

3. Spivack, *Shakespeare*, 240.

4. Brooke, "The Moral Tragedy of *Doctor Faustus*," 111.

5. Ibid., 118.

6. "There was a distinct feeling in the air that, though damnation was a certainty unless steps were taken to avert it, salvation was a problematical and tricky business. And there is plenty of evidence to suggest that Marlowe at Cambridge was thoroughly exposed to this opinion and the debates it provoked." Sanders, *Dramatist and the Received Idea*, 227.

7. As modern church historians have come to realize, hard and fast distinctions among believers are often impossible to achieve:

While many people to whom the term [puritan] is applied were in fact nonconformists or advocates of some sort of institutional reform of the church, not all of them were. Moreover, the slightly uneven not to say promiscuous, ways in which conformity was defined and enforced in the Elizabethan church often make it difficult to say whether or not an individual conformed, and, if he did, what that 'conformity' amounted to.

Since this view of puritanism is founded on a sense of a common core of religious experience and values, which could transcend the formal issues of conformity and church government, it is inevitably somewhat too loose and open-ended for comfort.
Lake, *Anglicans and Puritans?* 4–5.

8. Brigden, *London and the Reformation*, 268.

9. Dawley, *John Whitgift*, 216.

10. Collinson, *Elizabethan Puritan Movement*, 434; Collinson, *Religion of Protestants*, 6.

11. Dawley, *John Whitgift*, 217.

12. Tyacke, *Anti-Calvinists*, 4.

13. Ibid., 29.

14. Collinson, *Elizabethan Puritan Movement*, 434.

15. Urry, *Christopher Marlowe and Canterbury*, 55. See also Hardin, "Marlowe and the Fruits of Scholarism," 398, for a discussion of the intellectual life at Cambridge during Marlowe's student years and the conflict between "the practical and the spiritual ends of learning" that, in the case of Doctor Faustus, reflect "a frustrated search for wisdom."

16. New, *Anglican and Puritan*, 9.

17. For a discussion of the problems of dating the play, see Steane, *Marlowe*, 117–19.

18. Fuller, *Holy State*, 90. Fuller, who was a student at Sidney Sussex, may have heard this directly from Samuel Ward, who became master there.

19. Helyn, *Historia Quinqu-Articularis*, 66.

20. Perkins, *Works*, 43.

21. Porter, *Reformation and Reaction*, 376.

22. Helyn, *Historia Quingu-Articularis*, 66. See also the account in Lake, *Moderate Puritans*, 201–42.

23. William Empson speculates that an earlier and more heretical version of the play was suppressed by the master of the revels; though vigorously argued, his thesis has no documentary evidence. See John Henry Jones, ed., *Faustus and the Censor*. Janet Clare, *Art Made Tongue-tied*, considers the possibility that the Bruno scene in the B version "originated with Marlowe, part of it being suppressed before early performance but later recovered with some adulterations by Rowley."
Yet according to Clare the censorship of the 1616 edition went "beyond the strict prohibition of utterances taken as blasphemous" (i.e. the "Acte to restraine Abuses of Players" of 1606), for "several of the doctrinal allusions in the play" as well as

the omission of further short passages and lines . . . can reasonably be attributed to censorship in reference to the Act. . . . The manuscript underlying the 1616 edition of *Doctor Faustus* has, therefore, suffered thoroughgoing censorship in accordance with Jacobean legislation. . . . The extent and nature of the censorship of the 'B' text . . . suggest that, when the play was revived, revised, and augmented with the Rowely and Bird 'adycions' recorded by Henslowe, it was regarded as a new play, re-submitted to the Master of the Revels, and censored in accordance with recent legislation. . . . The 'Acte to restraine Abuses of Players' is itelf relatively limited in scope; but it would seem on the basis of the censorship of the 'B' text of *Doctor Faustus* that it could be invoked to sabotage plays which dealt liberally and critically with matters of scripture or doctrine, 104–5.

Although intriguing, all of this is, of course, highly speculative.

24. Perkins, *Works*, "A Discourse of the Damned Art of Witchcraft framed and delivered by Mr. William Perkins in his ordinary course of preaching" (1608), 581. And in her recent edition of the play, Roma Gill points out that in this work Perkins describes the "mental and spiritual deterioration" dramatized in the middle parts of the play: "When they first beginne to grow in confederacie with the devill, they are sober, and their understanding sound . . . but after they be once in the league . . . then reason and understanding may be depraved, memorie weakened and the powers of their soule blemished." Marlowe, *Doctor Faustus*, ed. by Gill. xxix–xxx.

25. Perkins, *Works*, 591.

26. In the prologue, the chorus uses the language of the university when describing Faustus as one "grac't with Doctors name," i.e. recorded in a "Grace Book." See Bakeless, *Christopher Marlowe*, 45.

27. All quotations are from *Marlowe, Doctor Faustus*, ed. by Greg. Unless otherwise noted, citations are from the 1604 version, for Michael Keefer has convincingly argued that it "represents a relatively more authentic version of the play." See Marlowe, *Doctor Faustus*, xii.

28. Helyn, *Historia Quingu-Articularis*, 66, see footnote 13.

29. Perkins, *Works*, 139.

30. Perkins, *Works*, 152–67.

31. Matalene finds that the hero "takes up each book in turn, not in order to attend to it (though that is what he pretends to do), but in order to hear himself draw automatically on a memorized fund of usually pejorative observations about it. Our first impression of Faustus' scholarly life is that it is a constant game of 'one-upmanship' with the great." "Marlowe's *Faustus*," 502.

32. "A Faithful and Plain Exposition upon Zephaniah 2. 1–2, delivered at Stourbridge Fair in 1593" (1605). Perkins, *Works*, 285.

33. Except for this citation, all my quotations from the play appear in *both* the 1604 and 1616 quartos. In a comparison of the A (1604) and B (1616) editions, Leah Marcus argues that the earlier is more Calvinistic. See her article, "Textual Indeterminacy."

34. Paul H. Kocher disagrees: "Faustus has free will, free capacity to repent. It is his own fault that he does not, and so he goes to a condign doom." *Christopher Marlowe*, 108. For a discussion of the place of magic in the play, see West, "Impatient Magic of Dr. Faustus."

35. *A Discourse of the Damned Art of Witchcraft*, in Perkins, *Works*, 593.

36. *Golden Chain*, 1591, in Perkins, *Works*, 123.

37. Porter, *Reformation and Reaction*, 381.

38. "Fragments of an Answer to the Letter of Certain English Protestants" in *Works*, Book V, Appendix 1, 537.

39. Porter, *Reformation and Reason*, 381.

40. See Hattaway, "Theology of Marlowe's *Doctor Faustus*."

41. Sanders, *Dramatist and the Received Idea*, 235.

42. "The Old Man's precepts concerning the continued amiability of Faustus's soul and the accessibility of grace reflect a scholastic and moderate Anglican emphasis upon the idea that the wicked render themselves incapable of salvation." Wilks, *Idea of Conscience*, 150.

43. As Michael Keefer has remarked in the introduction to his edition of

the play: "[Faustus's] perseverance in despair is as distinct a sign of divine reprobation as Calvin held perseverance in grace to be one of divine election, and the insistent suggestions of the A text that his repeated inability to will his own salvation is due to the workings of another will, anterior to his and subjecting him to its determinations, make Faustus's 'torture' deeply unsettling. A Calvinistic orthodoxy may appear to win out at the end of this play, but it does so at the cost of being exposed, in the moment of its triumph, as intolerable." Marlowe, *Doctor Faustus*, ed. by Keefer, xiv.

44. According to Pauline Honderich, in this speech "Marlowe calls up and sets against each other the images both of the benevolent God of the Catholic dispensation and of the harsh and revengeful God of Calvinist doctrine." See Honderich, "John Calvin and *Doctor Faustus*." But Stachniewski, *Persecutory Imagination*, takes issue with her view that "it is the devils who are Calvinists and that Faustus is guilty of 'an individual error' in accepting their theology." According to Stachniewski, "Taking this line . . . forces the play to point the dotty moral that God consigns Faustus to everlasting torment for the 'error' of failing to realize how merciful he is," 295, footnote 6.

45. Perkins, *Works*, 86.

46. *Golden Chain*, in ibid., 256. First published in Latin in 1590; in English in 1591.

47. Cross, *Church and People*, 98.

48. Collinson, *Religion of Protestants*, 202.

49. Macfarlane, "Tudor Anthropologist," 140–55.

50. Collinson, *Religion of Protestants*, 202.

51. See Jean Howard's discussion in "Renaissance Antitheatricality," 167.

52. Sinfield, *Literature in Protestant England*, 14.

53. Marlowe, *Doctor Faustus*, ed. by Gill, xxii.

54. Sinfield, *Faultlines*, 234.

55. After examining some twenty-four essays on *Dr. Faustus*, Max Bluestone determined that critical "opinion divides about equally between those who see the play as orthodox and those who see it as heterdox or ambiguous." "Libido Speculandi," 38, footnote 5.

56. Rabkin, *Shakespeare and the Common Understanding*.

57. Sanders, *Dramatist and the Received Idea*, 242.

58. Helyn, *Historia Quingu-Articularis*, 66.

59. Chambers, *Elizabethan Stage*, 4:306. See also the discussion in Patterson, *Shakespeare and the Popular Voice*, 18–28.

CHAPTER 3. *MEASURE FOR MEASURE:* SAINTS' LIVES AND "HEAVENLY COMFORTS"

1. Winwood, *Memorials of Affairs of State*, II:49.

2. Leah Marcus, focusing on quite different elements in its composition and on its possible contemporary analogues, also remarks on the play's "space of indefinition," 202. "Relocating English ecclesiastical practices within a space dominated by the Counter-English and Roman Catholic usage" it "equivocates between different imperial modes" "in a way that would have been profoundly

alienating for large segments of a London Protestant audience," 194–95. Marcus points out how James's behavior was similar to that of the Archduke Albert, the Habsburg governor of the Austrian Netherlands who had married the Infanta Isabella. Both men were insisting on "Roman law and equity in preference to local ordinance," (193) and James's peace with Spain and the Archdukes was hardly a popular move with militant Protestants worried by the inital actions of their new ruler. See Marcus, *Puzzling Shakespeare*, 160–202.

3. Dutton, *Mastering the Revels*, 86, 89, 178.

4. As Emrys Jones has observed, recent Shakespeare scholarship has tended to ignore or overlook the Renaissance theater's indebtedness to the religious drama of the later fourteenth and fifteenth centuries. *Origins of Shakespeare*, 31. Two exceptions are worthy of mentioning. A discussion of the ways that Catholic and pre-Reformation traditions were Protestantized so that the older hagiographical material could be transformed to serve the Protestant cause can be found in Gasper, *Dragon and the Dove*, 17. And John D. Cox speculates on the ways that the medieval dramatic tradition, as found in the N-town mystery cycle in particular, "can be taken as a paradigm . . . for the medieval dramatic background of *Measure for Measure*." "The Medieval Background," 3.

5. Wasson, "Secular Saint Plays," 241.

6. Schoenbaum, *Annals*; Jeffrey, "English Saint's Plays," 69.

7. For a discussion of the ways in which Bale's successors turned to Foxe's *Book of Martyrs* for both source material and a Protestant view of history, see Spikes, "Jacobean History Play." The most recent and extensive discussion will be found in White, *Theatre and Reformation*.

8. Belsey, "Case of Hamlet's Conscience," 130.

9. Wasson, "Secular Saint Plays," 243.

10. Shakespeare, *Measure for Measure*. All quotations are from the Arden edition, New York: Random House, 1965.

11. According to the Harbage-Schoenbaum, *Annals*, plays on the life of St. Katherine were performed from the eleventh to the fifteenth centuries in Dunstable, London, and Coventry.

12. According to the *Golden Legend*, after watching St Margaret endure her torments unscathed, "five thousand persons were converted, and were beheaded for professing the name of Christ," de Voragine, 354.

13. The Harbage-Schoenbaum, *Annals*, notes a performance of a lost St. Christopher play in Yorkshire "by strollers" in 1609.

14. The most commonly dramatized example was also one of the most popular of all saints in the Church calendar: St. Nicholas, whose story is told in its best known form in de Voragine, *Golden Legend*.

15. For a discussion of some aspects of medieval drama that are similar to those found in Shakespeare's play, see Cox, "Medieval Background."

16. Howard, "*Measure for Measure*," 150.

17. See David Stevenson's discussion of Isabella's spiritual growth in *Achievement of Shakespeare's "Measure for Measure*," 30, 49.

18. For scholarly discussion of religious issues and *Measure for Measure* see: Raymond Southall, "*Measure for Measure* and the Protestant Ethic;" Gless, *Measure for Measure, the Law, and the Convent*; Schleiner, "Providential Improvisation;" Spinrad, "*Measure for Measure* and the Art of Not Dying," Leggatt,

"Substitution in *Measure for Measure*;" Pinciss, " 'Heavenly Comforts of Despair.'

19. In the section on faith in the *Institutes of the Christian Religion*, Calvin wrote: only after the penitent "have divested themselves of all arrogance through recognition of their own poverty, have wholly cast themselves down, and have plainly become worthless to themselves, then at last they may begin to taste the sweetness of mercy which the Lord holds out to them." (63–64) For a discussion of the progression from despair to a state of "assurance of salvation" see Knappen, *Tudor Puritanism*, 393. As Rowland Wymer explains, "The sorrow for sin which could bring a person to despair was also a necessary first step to achieving a state of grace." *Suicide and Despair*, 6. For an allied discussion see Rozett, *Doctrine of Election*. Susan Snyder has pointed out: "The whole Protestant emphasis on man's complete unworthiness and helplessness tended to reinforce the paradox of despair, to make it at once more necessary and more terrible. Luther in particular, proceeding from his own past agonizings over the inadequacies of confession and penance and the awful justice of God, his sudden seizures and black despondencies, placed despair of self at the very core of Christian experience." "The Left Hand of God."

20. Snyder, "Left Hand of God," 28. William Tyndale, "Prologue Upon the Epistle of St. Paul to the Romans," *Doctrinal Treatises* as quoted in Wymer, *Suicide and Despair*, 6.

21. According to Article XVI of the Thirty-nine Articles, which defined the doctrines of faith of the Church of England:

> After we have received the Holy Ghost, we may depart from grace given, and fall into sin, and by the grace of God (we may) rise again and amend our lives. And therefore they are to be condemned which say, they can no more sin as long as they live here, or deny place of forgiveness to such as truly repent.

22. Cleaver, *Four Godlie and Fruitful Sermons*.

23. Perkins, *Works* I:455–69; *A treatise tending unto a declaration whether a man bee in the estate of damnation, or in the estate of grace....*

24. One can suggest a number of reasons why Shakespeare frequently presents characters who struggle with their despair: it was a concern of widespread interest for his audience; it often affected men in an extremely emotional and therefore highly dramatic manner; and since it is a subject of *Corinthians*, one of his favorite New Testament books, it may have attracted him personally.

25. A problematic work whose central character is a ruling duke disguised as a friar naturally raises questions about the nature of political power as well as religion. As a consequence this play is especially appealing to new historicists, for example Greenblatt, "Representing Power," and Tennenhouse, *Power on Display*. Other critical approaches continue to find the work congenial: the psychoanalytic in Skura, *Literary Uses of Psychoanalysis*, and the literary and symbolic in Hammond, "Argument of *Measure for Measure*," and Leggatt, "Substitution in *Measure for Measure*."

26. Schleiner, "Providential Improvisation," 227.

27. For a discussion of the Duke's character and a summary of critical judgments about him see Lewis, " 'Dark Deeds Darkly Answered.' "

28. For a discussion of the various attitudes toward death expressed in the play see Spinrad, "*Measure for Measure* and the Art of Not Dying."

29. Edwards, *Shakespeare and the Confines of Art,* 118.

30. Hawkins, *Measure for Measure,* 104–5.

31. Levine, "Duke Vincentio and Angelo," 268.

32. Edwards, *Shakespeare and the Confines of Art,* 118–119.

33. "The Second Part of the Homily of Repentance" in *Certain Sermons or Homilies.*

34. Douglas Peterson, *"Measure for Measure."*

35. R.A. Foakes notes that the Duke's advice "corresponds closely enough with the counsel of Despair in Spenser's *Faerie Queene." Shakespeare the Dark Comedies,* 22.

36. In his article "More Light on *Measure for Measure,"* Warren D. Smith finds, interestingly enough, that fourteen critics approve and thirteen disapprove of Isabella's conduct with her brother in this scene.

37. Lascelles, *Shakespeare's "Measure for Measure,"* 88.

38. Gless, *Measure for Measure, the Law, and the Convent,* 190.

39. Hooker, *Sermon on the Certainty,* 6.

CHAPTER 4. *WHEN YOU SEE ME YOU KNOW ME* AND *IF YOU KNOW NOT ME YOU KNOW NOBODY:* PROTESTANISM AND PURITAN PROPAGANDA

1. Foakes, *"Perkin Warbeck* and *King Henry VIII,"* 18.

2. Leggatt, *English Drama,* 178.

3. Though the king was crowned at Westminster Abbey on 25 July 1603, the royal procession through London was postponed because of the plague until 15 March 1604.

4. Mulryne, Introduction to *Theatre and Government,* Mulryne and Shewring, eds. 18. Although the Prince of Wales was an appropriate patron for Rowley's Protestant propaganda, the patroness of Heywood's company, Queen Anne, was not. Evidently, the repertory of an acting company was not always so closely coordinated with the politics of its patron.

5. Madeleine Doran in Heywood, *If You Know Not Me* Malone Society edition, xiv. All quotations from the play are from this edition.

6. Rowley, *When You See Me,* Malone Society edition, x. All quotations from the play are from this edition.

7. In the introduction F. P. Wilson notes that "Rowley had a strong Protestant bias," ibid., x.

8. Spikes, "Jacobean History Play." See especially 125.

9. Willson, *King James VI and I,* 274–75.

10. J. R. Mulryne points out that "the text refers extra-dramatically" to Prince Henry, for Rowley's Henry VIII asks Jane Seymour to be the mother of "a chopping boy . . . / Ad a ninth Henrie to the English Crowne / And thou mak'st full my hopes" (II. 265–68). "The 'ninth Henrie' in an audience's mind in 1604 or 1605 was surely the present prince, son to King James," Mulryne and Shrewing, *Theatre and Government,* 18.

11. Rowley, *When You See Me,* x.

12. Margot Heinemann in *"King Lear* and the World Upside Down," notes

that Rowley's version of Will Summers is "iconoclastic, egalitarian, anti-Popish . . . and a champion of the poor." The clown's comment that the poor "present Christ" whereas "the Pope is at best St. Peter's deputy" is an aphorism "traceable back to the Lollards," 81–82.

13. According to Julia Gasper "the description of Gardiner offered in Poynet's *Treatise on Politicke Power* gives some idea of the kind of being established in popular memory and imagination:

> This doctour had a swart colour, an hanging loke,
> frowning browes, eies an ynche within the head, a nose
> hooked like a bussarde, wyde nosetrilles like a horse,
> euer snuffing into the wynde, a sparowe mouthe, great
> pawes like the deuil, talaunts on his fete like a
> grype, two ynches longer than the naturall toes, and so
> tyed with sinowes, that he coulde not abyde to be
> touched, nor scarce suffre them to touche the stones.

Not the warmest account that one bishop of Winchester could give of another. The Jacobean companies would have had difficulty making him repulsive enough for popular taste in their stage portrayals." "Reformation Plays," 199.

14. See Barton, "King Disguised," 92–117 for an analysis of the ways this action is treated in plays of the period. She does not discuss this example.

15. Collinson, "Jacobean Religious Settlement," 29.

16. Perkins, *Works*, I.122 as quoted in Knappen, *Tudor Puritanism*, 355.

17. Lake, *Moderate Puritans*, 287.

18. Knappen, *Tudor Puritanism*, 355.

19. Collinson, *Elizabethan Puritan Movement*, 27.

20. Haller, *Elect Nation*, 52.

21. For studies of Puritan opposition to the stage see Thompson, *Controversy Between Puritans and the Stage*; Fraser, *War Against Poetry*; and Barish, *Antitheatrical Prejudice*.

22. For a discussion of Dekker's plays and pageants see Gasper, *Dragon and the Dove*; for Middleton see Heinemann, *Puritanism and Theatre*, especially 173–74 and 199.

23. See Heinemann, *Puritanism and Theatre*, 16–21 and 121–26.

24. Harbage, *Shakespeare's Audience*, 69.

25. Heinemann, *Puritanism and Theatre*, 76–77. Her definition of Puritanism is taken from Trevelyan; see 22.

26. In " 'God Help the Poor,' " Margot Heinemann observes that plays that emphasized the Protestant Reformation presented it as a "popular rather than an aristocratic movement. The common people are insistently shown as the principal supporters of 'the religion'. . . . The reformed religion has its aristocratic and gentry heroes in the drama—Lady Jane Grey, Sir Thomas Wyatt—but it is the images of plebian support that are most striking, based on nationalism and patriotism as much as religious doctrine," 154.

27. Bevington, *Tudor Drama and Politics*.

28. McLuskie, *Dekker and Heywood*, 44.

29. Margot Heinemann has pointed out that, "The Bible in English [as the] symbol of the reformed religion is a recurrent image. . . . This is not as uncontroversial as it looks, [for] it had political and democratic connotations. . . .

And there were those who thought a religion based on reading the Scriptures dangerous to the social order." "Political Drama," 198.

30. Osborn, ed., *Quenes Majesties Passage*, 44.

31. Ibid., 48.

32. Ibid., 64.

33. *When You See Me* was published in 1605 and reprinted in 1613, 1621, and 1632; *If You Know Not Me* was printed in 1605 and reprinted in 1606, 1608, 1610, 1613, 1623, 1632, and 1639.

34. McLuskie notes that Heywood revived the play in 1633 when it served "as an exemplar of militant Protestantism and a contrast to the politics of Charles I," *Dekker and Heywood*, 167.

35. Heineman, *Puritanism and Theatre*, 65–66.

36. Butler, *Theatre and Crisis*, 185.

37. Ibid., 201.

38. "[As plays that referred to] the sicknesses of the state and the possible political remedies . . . were established, repeated and revived such sentiments must have been continually before men's eyes; and at the Blackfriars, Phoenix, and Salisbury Court, where the audiences regularly included country gentlemen up in town, anxious about Ship Money, lawyers concerned about the legality of Charles's prerogative schemes, great merchants and businessmen whom Charles's monopolies and demands for credit had milked, representatives of the political nation who in a few years' time would be sitting again in parliament, their impact must have been immense." Ibid., 286.

CHAPTER 5. *BARTHOLOMEW FAIR* AND JONSONIAN TOLERANCE

1. Butler, "Ecclesiastical Censorship," 469. Butler is nicely restating the argument of Annabel Patterson in *Censorship and Interpretation*.

2. Jackson, *Vision and Judgment*, 55.

3. Jonson, *Bartholomew Fair*. All quotations are from Eugene Waith's edition, 1963.

4. Jonson, *Works*, Vol. x, 171.

5. I would argue that Busy and the Littlewit party are enough of a satire of Puritans for any play, but in David McPherson's view, Overdo is a composite satiric picture of, among others, "Puritans in general, and George Whetstone, Richard Johnson, and Mayor Thomas Middleton in particular, " 229. "Origins of Overdo."

6. Levin, Richard, "Structure of *Bartholomew Fair*," 175.

7. Wells, *Elizabethan and Jacobean Playwrights*, 205.

8. Dures, *English Catholicism*, 28.

9. *Middlesex Country Records* 1. 207. See also *Calendar of State Papers Domestic* 1591–4, 403, 528, and Bushell, "Bellamies of Uxendon."

10. Middlesex Record Office Acc. 853/13.

11. Finkelpearl, " 'Comedians' Liberty,' " 134.

12. For a discussion of Jonson's views on religion (which supports the read-

ing of *Bartholomew Fair* proposed here), see Norbrook, *Poetry and Politics.* See especially chap. 7, 175–77.

13. Dures, *English Catholicism,* 49–50.

14. Peter Lake, "Anti-popery." Although Northampton was no friend of Jonson's, both men would have welcomed an easing of Parliamentary penalties and restrictions. Jonson, the posthumous son of an Anglican minister, had been a Catholic convert for some nine years, returning to the Church of England in 1610, but throughout his life he maintained very warm friendships with such important and influential English Catholics as Esme Stuart, Duke of Lennox; William Parker, fourth Baron Monteagle; Sir Ralph Sheldon; and Sir Kenelm Digby.

15. See the discussion in Dures and in Bossy, *English Catholic Community.*

16. Waith, "John Ford," 12.

17. "The Fair, for one the symbol of everything carnal summed up in the word 'abomination,' is for the other the symbol of everything disorderly summed up in the term 'enormity,' " Barish, *Ben Jonson,* 209–10.

18. Manning, "Echo of King James."

19. The repetition of James's words is only one of many similarities between Overdo and the king to whom Jonson dedicated this play. Leah Marcus in *Politics of Mirth* thinks Overdo a "distorted shadow of James" and the play "a lucid and elegant defense of royal perogative," 55; 40. Keith Sturgess proposes that "in Overdo . . . the court might well have seen a burlesque portrait of James himself. Monarch and magistrate share a tendency towards pedantry, an easy familiarity with classical quotations, an urge to inveigh against tobacco and its evil effects, and even, perhaps, a notably protective attitude towards young favourites." *Jacobean Private Theatre,* 171.

20. "It is a location historically associated with harsh justice against religious nonconformists, both Catholic and Protestants, and with iconoclasm directed against the images associated with worship or devotion—iconoclasm that Busy would extend even further." Davidson, "Judgment, Iconoclasm," 352. I am indebted to Professor Davidson for the discussion that follows.

21. See Teague, *Curious History of Bartholomew Fair.* Cokes himself reminds us of these connections: "an' ever any Barthol'mew had that luck in't that I have had, I'll be martyred for him, and in Smithfield too" (IV.ii.65–66).

22. Davidson, "Judgment, Iconoclasm," 354.

23. For a discussion of the staging of the play, see R.B. Parker, "Themes and Staging of *Bartholomew Fair."*

24. Cope, Jackson, "Bartholomew Fair as *Blasphemy."*

25. 148.

26. Clifford Davidson agrees: "Such a model does not quite fit the play," "Judgment, Iconoclasm," ft. 3, 349–50.

27. Salingar, "Crowd and Public in *Bartholomew Fair,"* 149–50. In place of these readings Salingar proposes that the play's "underlying theme is London society considered as a literary or theatrical public," 151. But this takes no notice of the varied religious and moral positions of the assorted characters.

28. Thomas Cartelli, "*Bartholomew Fair* as Urban Arcadia," 154–55. Cartelli points out that most Jonson scholars have commented on this, including Barish, *Language of Prose Comedy,* 187–239; Richard Levin; and John Enck in *Jonson and the Comic Truth,* 189–208. Leo Salingar also remarks that Jonson's

"tone here is ironic gaiety rather than an earnest spirit of satiric correction." "Crowd and Public," 149.

29. Barton, *Names of Comedy*, 79. Gabriele Jackson also notes that for Jonson's characters "there are indeed essential qualities in names which can be intuitively perceived," *Vision and Judgment*, 58.

30. Hamel, "Order and Judgment," 53. Hamel is one of the rare critics of the play to have a just appreciation for Grace's virtues.

31. Perhaps it is worth noting that in the action of the play Grace is not much involved with Rabbi Busy. As an explanation we could point out that the Puritan emphasis on predestination left little room for the operation of grace.

32. Naturally, if Cokes is a Catholic, Dame Overdo might also belong to the same church as her brother. In that case, of course, she would not practice the same religion as her husband. Although such questions move us rather far from Jonson's play and its invented characters, such marriages were not uncommon. In fact, John Bossy, *English Catholic Community*, has found that in Elizabethan-Jacobean marriages there was a "high incidence of conformable husbands with recusant wives. . . . A lot of Protestant or conformist gentlemen had Catholic wives around 1600," 154–55. "All in all, I think the evidence entitles us to conclude that, to a considerable degree, the Catholic community owed its existence to gentlewomen's dissatisfaction at the Reformation settlement of religion, and that they played an abnormally important part in its early history. This matriarchal era, if one may call it so, seems to have come to an end about 1620," 158.

33. Salingar, "Crowd and Public," 148; Cope, Jackson, "*Bartholomew Fair* as Blasphemy," 146.

34. Donaldson, *World Upside-Down*, 55.

35. George Rowe makes a slightly different case, arguing that Jonson does not seek to prove equality among religious positions but rather "presents as devastating a critique of various claims to authority as *The Clouds* directs at Socrates." *Distinguishing Jonson*, 147.

CHAPTER 6. *PERKIN WARBECK* AND THE POLITICS OF 1632

1. Ross, *Winter Queen*, 28.
2. *Calendar of State Papers Venetian* 9 July 1620.
3. *Calendar of State Papers Domestic*, 20 February 1620.
4. *Stuart Royal Proclamations*. No. 208: 495–96.
5. Ross, *Winter Queen*, 78–79. As Annabel Patterson describes it, "Elizabeth . . . became for England a symbol of Protestantism left in the lurch," *Censorship and Interpretation*, 75.
6. Gasper, *Dragon and the Dove*, 202.
7. Wedgwood, *Thirty Years War*, 129.
8. Oman, *Elizabeth of Bohemia*, 291.
9. Green, *Elizabeth of Bohemia*, 277.
10. Barbara Lewalski notes: "Over the years [the Countess of Bedford] promoted the cause of the Elector Palatine and the Electress Elizabeth . . . whose plight became a *cause celebre* in the struggles of international Protestantism against Rome and Spain. In 1621 she made a hazardous sea voyage to visit

Elizabeth in the Hague and frequently wrote news and advice to her." "Lucy, Countess of Bedford," 55.

11. Sharpe, ed. *Faction and Parliament*, 139.

12. Oman, *Elizabeth of Bohemia*, 327.

13. Limon, *Dangerous Matter*, 40–61.

14. Gasper, *Dragon and the Dove*, 190.

15. Patterson, *Censorship and Interpretation*, 86.

16. Gasper, *Dragon and the Dove*, 9. Chapter 3 offers an extensive discussion.

17. In *True History of the Earl of Tyrone* (1619), Thomas Gainsford remarks: "How Perkin Warbeck . . . went forward . . . against the house of Lancaster, our stages of London have instructed those which cannot read." See John J. O'Connor, "A Lost Play of Perkin Warbeck," *Modern Language Notes* LXX (1955): 566. In Appendix III of his edition of Ford's *The Chronicle History of Perkin Warbeck A Strange Truth* (Manchester: Manchester University Press, 1968), Peter Ure considers this possibility. I have used this text for all quotations from the play.

18. Judith Anderson discusses how important an issue in this play is "the relation of words to reality," 173. In her view, Ford's poetry has established Warbeck's claims in ways that "have surpassed those found in any of the histories from which Ford drew his play. Poetic words have imparted a presence to him that the matter of history cannot match, and in doing so, they have made the play relevant to a modern materialism," 190–91. Ultimately, she argues, "Ford's *Perkin* . . . [is able] to challenge the truth of chronicle itself," 194, ft. 13. "'But We Shall Teach the Lad Another Language': History and Rhetoric in Bacon, Ford, and Donne," *Renaissance Drama* N.S. 20 (1989): 169–96.

19. *Essays on Elizabethan Drama* (New York: Harcourt, Brace and Company, 1932), 136.

20. In 1625 the Queen's Men began performing at the Phoenix, where they presented four of Ford's plays.

21. Drama is not the only art form that takes up these matters. Kevin Sharpe argues that Aurelian Townshend's "Elegy on the death of the King of Sweden: sent to Thomas Carew" also urges more forceful English intervention. In November 1632, Gustavus Adolphus, the King of Sweden, who "had stood in the eyes of the 'hotter' Protestants of England and Europe as the hope for the defeat of the Habsburg Antichrist and for the triumph of the Protestant cause," was killed at the battle of Lutzen. "Townshend's poem . . . must be read as a forthright criticism of Charles I's neutrality. . . . The poet spurs Charles to bear Gustavus's shield . . . and so to succeed to the King of Sweden's fame and immortality," *Criticism and Compliment The politics of literature in the England of Charles I* (Cambridge: Cambridge University Press, 1987), 175.

22. Butler, *Theatre and Crisis*, 195.

23. Ibid., 198.

24. Cavendish himself "wrote plays which were appeals for the restoration of Elizabethan modes." Sharpe, *Criticism and Compliment*, 18.

25. Barton, "He That Plays the King," 78–79.

26. Edwards, *Threshold of A Nation*, 185.

27. "All of Ford's sources conclude the tale of Perkin with an account of his confession. . . . Hall and Gainsford reprint the confession in full, and it is

remarkably circumstantial. Ford's departure from this crucial event, far from being an attempt to *avoid* a conflict with history, constitutes a most audacious attempt to *provoke* one. It serves notice on us . . . that we are not to equate the Perkin of the play with the vulgar upstart of the historians." Barish, "*Perkin Warbeck*," 154.

28. Perhaps we should do well to remember that a "pretender" according to the OED is "a claimant to a throne or the office of a ruler; originally in a neutral sense, but now always applied to a claimant who is held to have no just title." This means that on the one hand, a "pretender," may be simply "one who puts forth a claim, or who aspires to or aims at something;" yet on the other hand, in more modern usage he may be "one who makes baseless pretensions." Ford, it seems, draws on both senses of the word to sustain the ambiguity of Warbeck's true origins.

29. Wedgwood, *Thirty Years War*, 131–32.

30. Ross, *Winter Queen*, 95.

31. Geoffrey Parker, *Thirty Years' War*, 52.

32. Wedgwood, *Thirty Years War*, 52–53.

33. Ibid., 149. Wedgwood continues: "It was Elizabeth who wrote voluminously to all the unofficial powers, her father's favourite and the leading courtiers of France, Elizabeth who tactfully christened her new-born daughter Louisa Hollandina and asked the Dutch States to be godfathers, Elizabeth who dazzled ambassadors and substituted the currency of her favours for the money which her husband had not got."

34. Ford, *Chronicle History of Perkin Warbeck*, xl–xli.

35. Bacon, *History of the Reign of King Henry VII*, 180.

36. Ford, *Perkin Warbeck*, edited by Anderson, xi.

37. As Eugene M. Waith observes, "The love of Perkin and Katherine is a prime ingredient in the paradoxical transformation of the imposter, Perkin, into a transcendental hero." "John Ford," 198.

38. The role played by Katherine's rejected suitor Lord Dalyell resembles that played in real life by William, Earl Craven (1601–97) who fought in support of Frederick and Elizabeth, joined the exiled queen's court at the Hague, and "in prosperity as in adversity . . . remained faithful to the service of the queen of Bohemia." *Dictionary of National Biography*, 48. Ford's closeness to those who supported Frederick and Elizabeth is further substantiated by his dedication of *The Broken Heart* (1629) to Lord Craven.

39. Michael Neill, analyzing the play as a "tragedy of manners," argues that such references to "the player as playing-card king" or queen relate to the work's "celebration of the actor as hero and its elevation of style as an absolute moral principle." " 'Anticke Pageantrie,' " 118.

40. Wedgwood, *Thirty Years War*, 108, 121.

41. For example, in 1623, in an attempt to further the marriage negotiations between Prince Charles and the Infanta of Spain, King James, to demonstrate his good faith, withdrew the English garrison from the fortress of Frankenthal, his son-in-law's last stronghold in Germany. Wedgwood, *Thirty Years War*, 180.

42. Lisa Hopkins argues that *Perkin Warbeck* reveals Ford as a dramatist of "disaffected aristocracy," 63. Since "the English and Scottish lords feature[d] prominently in Ford's play . . . all behave with remarkable dignity, courage, and uprightness" and since "there were strong family links between the fif-

teenth-century noblemen of the play and the seventeenth-century noblemen and women to whom he offered dedications," 40, in "this account of Tudor history . . . Charles I is being delicately but firmly reminded that his ancestors owed their thrones to the loyalty, resourcefulness and military prowess of their nobility, and that the nobility therefore deserves a suitable reward by being fully included and consulted in the process of the government," 50. Moreover, Ford may have "actually believed Perkin Warbeck to have been the rightful Richard of York," 60, and so "the play . . . could be seen as containing a reminder that such a thing [as usurpation] is possible—and that the support of the nobility would then be needed to avert it," 62. *John Ford's Political Theatre*.

CHAPTER 7. CONCLUSION: "WHERE TRUTH IS HID"

1. See the discussion in Sinfield, *Literature in Protestant England*, 118–19.
2. Mullaney, "Mourning and Misogyny," 143.
3. Lake, "Anti-popery," 72–106.

Bibliography

Ali, Florence. *Opposing Absolutes Conviction and Convention in John Ford's Plays*. Salzburg: Salzburg Studies in English Literature, 1974.

Altman, Joel. *The Tudor Play of Mind*. Berkeley: University of California Press, 1978.

Anderson, Donald K. Jr., ed. *"Concord in Discord" The Plays of John Ford 1586–1986*. New York: AMS Press, Inc., 1986.

———. *John Ford*. New York: Twayne Publishers, Inc., 1972.

Anderson, Judith H. " 'But We Shall Teach the Lad Another Language:' History and Rhetoric in Bacon, Ford, and Donne," *Renaissance Drama*, n.s., 20 (1989), 169–96.

Bacon, Francis. *History of the Reign of King Henry VII*. Edited by F. J. Levy. New York: Bobbs-Merrill Co., Inc., 1972.

Bakeless, John. *Christopher Marlowe: The Man and His Time*. New York: Washington Square Press, 1964.

Barish, Jonas A. *The Antitheatrical Prejudice*. Berkeley: University of California Press, 1981.

———. *Ben Jonson and the Language of Prose Comedy*. Cambridge: Harvard University Press, 1970.

———. *"Perkin Warbeck as Anti-History."* *Essays in Criticism* 20:2 (April 1970), 151–71.

Barton, Anne. "He That Plays the King: Ford's *Perkin Warbeck* and the Stuart History Play." In *English Drama: Forms and Development Essays in Honour of Muriel Clara Bradbrook*, edited by Marie Axton and Raymond Williams. Cambridge: Cambridge University Press, 1977.

———. "The King Disguised: Shakespeare's *Henry V* and the Comical History." In *The Triple Bond*, edited by Joseph G. Price. University Park: Pennsylvania State University Press, 1975.

———. *The Names of Comedy*. Toronto: University of Toronto Press, 1990.

Belsey, Catherine. "The Case of Hamlet's Conscience." *Studies in Philology* 76:2 (Spring 1979): 127–48.

Bergeron, David. "Elizabeth's Coronation Entry (1559): New Manuscript Evidence." *English Literary Renaissance* 8:1 (Winter 1978), 3–8.

Bevington, David. *Tudor Drama and Politics*. Cambridge: Harvard University Press, 1968.

Bluestone, Max. "Libido Speculandi" in *Reinterpretations of Elizabethan Drama*, New York: Columbia University Press, 1969.

Bossy, John. *The English Catholic Community, 1570–1850*. New York: Oxford University Press, 1976.

Breitenberg, Mark. " '. . . the hole matter opened:' Iconic Representation and Interpretation in 'The Quenes Majesties Passage.' " *Criticism* 28:1 (Winter 1986): 1–25.

Bridenbaugh, Carl. *Vexed and Troubled Englishmen 1590–1642*. New York: Oxford University Press, 1968.

Brigden, Susan. *London and the Reformation*. Oxford: Clarendon Press, 1989.

Brooke, Nicholas. "The Moral Tragedy of *Doctor Faustus*." Cambridge Journal 5 (1951–52). Reprinted in Jump, John, ed., *Marlowe Doctor Faustus: A Casebook*. London: Macmillan and Co., 1969.

Bueler, Lois E. "Role-Splitting and Reintegration: The Tested Woman Plot in Ford," *Studies in English Literature* 20:2 (Spring 1980): 325–44.

Burt, Richard. *Licensed by Authority: Ben Jonson and the Discourses of Censorship*. Ithaca: Cornell University Press, 1993.

Bushell, W. D. "The Bellamies of Uxendon." *Harrow Octocentary Tracts* 14 (n.d.).

Butler, Martin. "Ecclesiastical Censorship of Early Stuart Drama: The Case of Jonson's *The Magnetic Lady*." *Modern Philology* 89:4 (May 1992), 469–81.

———. *Theatre and Crisis, 1632–1642*. Cambridge: Cambridge Univerity Press, 1984.

Calendar of State Papers, Domestic (1547–1625), edited by Robert Lemon and M. A. E. Green. 12 volumes, 1856–72. London: Longman, Brown, Green, Longmans and Roberts.

Calendar of State Papers, Venetian (1202–1668), edited by Rawdon Brown, G. C. Bentinck, H. F. Brown, and H. B. Hinds. 35 volumes, 1864–1935. London: Longman, Brown, Green, Longmans and Roberts.

Calvin, John. *Institutes of the Christian Religion*, translated and annotated by Ford Lewis Battles. Grand Rapids: William B. Erdmans, 1986.

Candido, Joseph. "The 'Strange Truth' of *Perkin Warbeck*." *Philological Quarterly* 59:3 (Summer 1980): 300–16.

Carlton, Charles. *Archbishop William Laud*. New York: Routledge Kegan Paul, 1987.

Cartelli, Thomas. "*Bartholomew Fair* as Urban Arcadia." *Renaissance Drama*, n.s., 14 (1983): 151–72.

Certain Sermons or Homilies Appointed to be Read in Churches in the Time of the Late Queen Elizabeth, 1623. Gainesville: Scholars' Facsimiles & Reprints, 1968.

Chambers, E. K. *The Elizabethan Stage*. 4 vols. Reprint, 1961 Oxford: Clarendon Press, 1923.

Clare, Janet. *Art Made Tongue-tied by Authority*. New York: Manchester University Press, 1990.

Cleaver, Robert. *Four Godlie and Fruitful Sermons: Two Preached at Draiton in Oxfordshire*. N.p., 1611.

Clegg, Cyndia Susan. *Press Censorship in Elizabethan England*. Cambridge: Cambridge University Press, 1997.

Cole, Douglas. *Suffering and Evil in the Plays of Christopher Marlowe.* Princeton: Princeton University Press, 1962.

Collinson, Patrick. *The Elizabethan Puritan Movement.* Berkeley: University of California Press, 1967.

————. "The Jacobean Religious Settlement: The Hampton Court Conference." In *Before the English Civil War,* edited by Howard Tomlinson. London: Macmillan Press, 1983.

————. *The Religion of Protestants: The Church in English Society, 1559–1625.* Oxford: Clarendon Press, 1982.

Cope, Esther S. *Politics Without Parliaments, 1629–1640.* Boston: Allen & Unwin, 1976.

Cope, Jackson. "*Bartholomew Fair* as Blasphemy." *Renaissance Drama* 8 (1965): 127–52.

Cox, John D. "The Medieval Background of *Measure for Measure*." *Modern Philology* 81:1 (August 1983): 1–13.

Cross, Claire. *Church and People, 1450–1660.* Atlantic Highlands: Humanities Press, 1976.

Davidson, Clifford. "Judgment, Iconoclasm, and Anti-Theatricalism in Jonson's *Bartholomew Fair.*" *Papers on Language and Literature* 25:1 (Winter 1989): 349–63.

Dawley, Powell Mills. *John Whitgift and the English Reformation.* New York: Charles Scribner's Sons, 1954.

Dickens, A. G. *The English Reformation.* London: B.T. Batsford, Ltd, 1989.

Dollimore, Jonathan. *Radical Tragedy.* Chicago: University of Chicago Press, 1984.

Donaldson, Ian. *The World Turned Upside Down.* Oxford: Clarendon Press, 1970.

Dunn, Richard. *The Age of Religious Wars, 1559–1689.* New York: Norton, 1970.

Dures, Alan. *English Catholicism, 1558–1642.* Essex: Longman, 1983.

Dutton, Richard. *Mastering the Revels.* Iowa City: University of Iowa Press, 1991.

Edwards, Philip. *Shakespeare and the Confines of Art.* London: Methuen & Co., Ltd., 1968.

————. *Threshold of A Nation: A Study in English and Irish Drama.* Cambridge: Cambridge University Press, 1979.

Eliot, T. S. *Essays on Elizabethan Drama.* New York: Harcourt, Brace and Company, 1932.

Enck, John. *Jonson and the Comic Truth.* Madison: University of Wisconsin Press, 1966.

Farr, Dorothy M. *John Ford and the Caroline Theatre.* New York: Harper & Row, 1979.

Finkelpearl, Philip J. " 'The Comedians' Liberty:' Censorship of the Jacobean Stage Reconsidered." *English Literary Renaissance* 16:1 (Winter 1986), 123–38.

———. *Court and Country: Politics in the Plays of Beaumont and Fletcher*. Princeton: Princeton University Press, 1990.

Foakes, R. A. "*Perkin Warbeck* and *King Henry VIII*." *The Listener* 4 (August 1977): 18–19.

———. *Shakespeare the Dark Comedies to the Last Plays: From Satire to Celebration*. Charlottesville: University of Virginia Press, 1971.

Foster, Verna Ann. "*Perkin* Without the Pretender: Reexamining the Dramatic Center of Ford's Play." *Renaissance Drama* 16 (1985), 141–58.

Foxe, John. *Acts and Monuments of These Latter and Perilous Days*, edited by Stephen Read Cattley. 8 volumes. London, 1837–1841.

Fraser, Russell. *The War Against Poetry*. Princeton: Princeton University Press, 1970.

Freer, Coburn. " 'The Fate of Worthy Expectation:' Eloquence in *Perkin Warbeck*." In *'Concord in Discord' The Plays of John Ford, 1586–1986*, edited by Donald K. Anderson, Jr. New York: AMS Press Inc., 1986.

Fuller, Thomas. *The Holy State and the Profane State*. Cambridge, 1642.

Gainsford, Thomas. *The True and Wonderfull History of Perkin Warbeck*. London, 1618.

Gasper, Julia. *The Dragon and the Dove: The Plays of Thomas Dekker*. Oxford: Clarendon Press, 1990.

———. "The Reformation Plays on the Public Stage." In *Theatre and Government Under the Early Stuarts*, edited by J. R. Mulryne and Margaret Shrewing. Cambridge: Cambridge University Press, 1993.

Gless, Darryl J. *Measure for Measure, the Law, and the Convent*. Princeton: Princeton University Press, 1979.

Gorst-Williams, Jessica. *Elizabeth The Winter Queen*. London: Abelard, 1977.

Green, M. A. *Elizabeth of Bohemia*. Revised by S. C. Lomas. London: Methuen and Co., 1909.

Greenblatt, Stephen. "General Introduction." In *The Norton Shakespeare*, Stephen Greenblatt, general editor. New York: W.W. Norton Co., Inc., 1997.

———. "Representing Power: *Measure for Measure* in its Time." In *The Power of Forms in the English Renaissance* edited by Leonard Tennenhouse. Norman: University of Oklahoma Press, 1982.

———. *Shakespearean Negotiations*. Berkeley: University of California Press, 1988.

Gregg, Pauline. *King Charles I*. Berkeley: University of California Press, 1981.

Gurr, Andrew. *Playgoing in Shakespeare's London*. Cambridge: Cambridge University Press, 1987.

———. "Singing Through the Chatter: John Ford and Contemporary Theatrical Fashion." In *John Ford Critical Re-Visions*, edited by Michael Neill. Cambridge: Cambridge University Press, 1988.

Haller, William. *The Elect Nation: The Meaning and Relevance of Foxe's Book of Martyrs*. New York: Harper and Row, 1963.

Hamel, Guy. "Order and Judgment in *Bartholomew Fair*." *University of Toronto Quarterly* 43:1 (Fall 1973), 48–67.

Hammond, Paul. "The Argument of *Measure for Measure*." *English Literary Renaissance* 16 (Autumn 1986): 496–519.

Harbage, Alfred. *Annals of English Drama*, revised by S. Schoenbaum. London: Metheun & Co., 1964.

———. *Shakespeare's Audience*. New York: Columbia University Press, 1941.

Hardin, Richard. "Marlowe and the Fruits of Scholarism." *Philological Quarterly* 63:3 (Summer 1984): 387–400.

Hattaway, Michael. "The Theology of Marlowe's *Doctor Faustus*." *Renaissance Drama*, n.s., 3 (1970): 51–78.

Hawkins, Harriett. *Measure for Measure*: *Twayne's New Critical Introductions*. Boston: Twayne, 1987.

Heinemann, Margot, " 'God Help the Poor: the Rich Can Shift:' The World Upside-Down and the Popular Tradition in the Theatre." In *The Politics of Tragicomedy*, edited by Gordon McMullan and Jonathan Hope. New York: Routledge, 1992.

———. "*King Lear* and the World Upside Down." *Shakespeare Survey* 44 (1992): 75–83.

———. "Political Drama." In *The Cambridge Companion to English Renaissance Drama*, edited by A. R. Braunmuller and Michael Hattaway. Cambridge: Cambridge University Press, 1990.

———. *Puritanism and Theatre*: *Thomas Middleton and Opposition Drama Under the Early Stuarts*. Cambridge: Cambridge University Press, 1980.

Helyn, Peter. *Historia Quinqu-Articularis or*: *A Declaration of the Judgment of the Western Church*. London, 1660.

Holderness, B. A. *Pre-Industrial England*: *Economy and Society, 1500–1700*. Totowa, New Jersey: Rowman and Littlefield, 1976.

Honderich, Pauline. "John Calvin and *Doctor Faustus*." *Modern Language Review* 68:1 (January 1973): 1–13.

Hooker, Thomas. *Sermon on the Certainty and Perpetuity of Faith in the Elect*. In *Of the Laws of Ecclesiastical Polity*. Vol 1. New York: Dutton, 1907.

———. Fragments of an Answer to the Letter of Certain English Protestants. Vol. 11. Appendix I. New York: Dutton, 1907.

Hopkins, Lisa. *John Ford's Political Theatre*. Manchester: Manchester University Press, 1994.

Howard, Jean. " 'Effeminately Dolent:' Gender and Legitimacy in Ford's *Perkin Warbeck*." In *John Ford Critical Re-Visions*, edited by Michael Neill. Cambridge: Cambridge University Press, 1988.

———. "*Measure for Measure* and the Restraints of Convention." *Essays in Literature* 10:2 (Fall 1983), 149–58.

———. "Renaissance Antitheatricality and the Politics of Gender and Rank in *Much Ado About Nothing*." In *Shakespeare Reproduced*: *The Text in History and Ideology*, edited by Jean Howard and Marion O'Connor. New York: Methuen, 1987.

Howard-Hill, T. H., ed. *Shakespeare and Sir Thomas More*. Cambridge: Cambridge University Press, 1989.

Huebert, Ronald. " 'An Artificial Way to Grieve:' The Forsaken Woman in

Beaumont and Fletcher, Massinger and Ford." *English Literary Renaissance* 44:4 (Winter 1977): 601–21.

Jackson, Gabriele Bernhard. *Vision and Judgment in Ben Jonson's Drama*. New Haven: Yale University Press, 1968.

Jacobus de Voragine. *The Golden Legend*. New York: Longmans, Green, 1941.

Jeffrey, David L. "English Saint's Plays." In *Medieval Drama* edited by Neville Denny. London: Edward Arnold, 1973.

Jones, Emrys. *The Origins of Shakespeare*. Oxford: Clarendon Press, 1977.

Jones, John Henry, ed. *Faustus and the Censor*. Oxford: Basil Blackwell, 1987.

Kendall, Ritchie D. *The Drama of Dissent: The Radical Politics of Nonconformity, 1380–1590*. Chapel Hill: University of North Carolina Press, 1986.

Knappen, M. M. *Tudor Puritanism*. Chicago: University of Chicago Press, 1939.

Kocher, Paul H. *Christopher Marlowe: A Study of His Thought, Learning, and Character*. Chapel Hill: University of North Carolina Press, 1946.

Lake, Peter. *Anglicans and Puritans? Presbyterianism and English Conformist Thought from Whitgift to Hooker*. Boston: Allen and Unwin, 1988.

———. "Anti-popery: The Structure of a Prejudice." In *Conflict in Early Stuart England*, edited by Richard Cust and Ann Hughes. New York: Longman, 1989.

———. *Moderate Puritans and the Elizabethan Church*. Cambridge: Cambridge University Press, 1982.

Lascelles, Mary. *Shakespeare's "Measure for Measure."* London: University of London, 1953.

Leggatt, Alexander. *English Drama: Shakespeare to the Restoration, 1590–1660*. New York: Longman, 1988.

———. "Substitution in *Measure for Measure*." *Shakespeare Quarterly* 39 (Autumn 1988): 342–59.

Levin, Richard. "The Structure of *Bartholomew Fair*." *PMLA* 80:3 (June 1965): 172–79.

Levin, Richard A. "Duke Vincentio and Angelo: Would 'A Feather Turn the Scale'?" *Studies in English Literature* 22 (Spring 1982): 257–70.

Lewalski, Barbara. "Lucy, Countess of Bedford: Images of a Jacobean Courtier and Patroness." In *The Politics of Discourse*, edited by Kevin Sharpe and Steven Zwicker. Berkeley: University of California Press, 1987.

Lewis, Cynthia. " 'Dark Deeds Darkly Answered:' Duke Vincentio and Judgment in *Measure for Measure*." *Shakespeare Quarterly* 34 (Autumn 1983): 271–89.

Limon, Jerzy. *Dangerous Matter: English Drama and Politics in 1623/24*. Cambridge: Cambridge Unversity Press, 1986.

Macfarlane, Alan. "A Tudor Anthropologist: George Gifford's *Discourses* and *Dialogue*." In *The Damned Art: Essays in the Literature of Witchcraft*, edited by Sydney Anglo. London: Routledge Kegan Paul, 1977.

Manning, Gillian. "An Echo of King James in Jonson's *Bartholomew Fair*." *Notes and Queries*, n.s., 36:3 (September 1989): 342–44.

Marcus, Leah. *The Politics of Mirth*. Chicago: The University of Chicago Press, 1986.

———. *Puzzling Shakespeare Local Reading and Its Discontents*. Berkeley: University of California Press, 1988.

———. "Textual Indeterminacy and Ideological Difference: The Case of *Dr. Faustus*." *Renaissance Drama* 20 (1989): 1–29.

Matalene, H. W. III. "Marlowe's *Faustus* and the Comforts of Academicism." *English Literary History* 39:4 (December 1972): 495–519.

McLuskie, Kathleen E. *Dekker and Heywood*. New York: St. Martin's Press, 1994.

McMillan, Scott, *The Elizabethan Theatre and the Book of Sir Thomas More*. Ithaca: Cornell University Press, 1987.

McMullan, Gordon and Jonathan Hope, eds. *The Politics of Tragicomedy Shakespeare and After*. New York: Routledge, 1992.

McPherson, David. "The Origins of Overdo: A Study in Jonsonian Invention." *Modern Language Quarterly* 37:3 (September 1976): 221–33.

Middlesex County Records, ed. J. C. Jeaffreson, 4 V., 1886–92.

Middlesex Record Office Accounts. Middlesex Historical Commission, n.d.

Mullaney, Steven. "Mourning and Misogyny: *Hamlet*, The Revenger's Tragedy, and the Final Progress of Elizabeth I, 1600–1607." *Shakespeare Quarterly* 45 (Fall 1994): 139–62.

———. *The Place of the Stage*: *License, Play, and Power in Renaissance England*. Chicago: University of Chicago Press, 1988.

Mulryne, J. R. and Margaret Shrewing, eds. *Theatre and Government Under the Early Stuarts*. Cambridge: Cambridge University Press, 1993.

Neill, Michael. " 'Anticke Pageantrie' The Mannerist Art of *Perkin Warbeck*." *Renaissance Drama*, n.s., 7. (1976): 117–50.

New, John F. H. *Anglican and Puritan*: *The Basis of Their Opposition, 1558–1640*. Stanford, California: Stanford University Press, 1964.

Norbrook, David. " 'The Masque of Truth:' Court Entertainments and International Protestant Politics in the Early Stuart Period." *The Seventeenth Century* 1:2 (1986): 81–110.

———. *Poetry and Politics in the English Renaissance*. London: Routledge Kegan Paul, 1984.

O'Connor, John J. "A Lost Play of *Perkin Warbeck*." *Modern Language Notes* 70 (1955).

Oman, Carola. *Elizabeth of Bohemia*. London: Hodder and Stoughton, Ltd., 1938.

Orbison, Tucker. *The Tragic Vision of John Ford*. Salzburg: Salzburg Studies in English Literature, 1974.

Osborn, James M., ed. *The Quenes Majesties Passage Through the City of London*. 1559. New Haven: Yale University Press, 1960.

Owens, W. R., ed. *Seventeenth-Century England*: *A Changing Culture*. Totowa, New Jersey: Barnes and Noble, 1981.

Parker, Geoffrey. *The Thirty Years' War*. Boston: Routledge Kegan Paul, 1984.

Parker, R. B. "The Themes and Staging of *Bartholomew Fair*." *University of Toronto Quarterly* 39:4 (July 1970): 293–309.

Parry, Graham. *The Seventeenth Century: The Intellectual and Cultural Context of English Literature, 1603–1700*. New York: Longman, 1989.

Patterson, Annabel. *Censorship and Interpretation: The Conditions of Writing and Reading in Early Modern Europe*. Madison: University of Wisconsin Press, 1984.

———. *Shakespeare and the Popular Voice*. Oxford: Basil Blackwell, 1989.

Pearl, Valerie. *London and the Outbreak of the Puritan Revolution*. London: Oxford University Press, 1961.

Perkins, William. *The Works of William Perkins*, edited by Ian Breward. Abingdon: Sutton Courtenay Press, 1970.

Peterson, Douglas. "*Measure for Measure* and the Anglican Doctrine of Contrition." *Notes and Queries*, n.s., 11:4 (April 1964): 135–37.

Pinciss, G. M. "*Bartholomew Fair* and Jonsonian Tolerance." *Studies in English Literature*, 35:2 (Spring 1995).

———. " 'Heavenly Comforts of Despair' and *Measure for Measure*." *Studies in English Literature* 30:2 (Spring 1990): 303–13.

———. "Marlowe's Cambridge Years and the Writing of *Dr Faustus*." *Studies in English Literature* 33:2 (Spring 1993): 249–64.

Porter, H. C. *Reformation and Reaction in Tudor Cambridge*. Cambridge: Cambridge University Press, 1958.

Rabkin, Norman. *Shakespeare and the Common Understanding*. New York: The Free Press, 1967.

Randall, Dale B. J. " 'Theatres of Greatness:' A Revisionary View of Ford's *Perkin Warbeck*." Victoria: University of Victoria, 1986.

Ross, Josephine. *The Winter Queen: The Story of Elizabeth Stuart*. New York: St. Martin's Press, 1979.

Rowe, George. *Distinguishing Jonson: Imitation, Rivalry, and the Direction of a Dramatic Career*. Lincoln: University of Nebraska Press, 1988.

Rozett, Martha Tuck. *The Doctrine of Election and the Emergence of Elizabethan Tragedy*. Princeton: Princeton University Press, 1984.

Russell, Conrad. *The Crisis of Parliaments*. London: Oxford University Press, 1971.

———, ed. *The Origins of the English Civil War*. New York: Harper and Row, 1973.

Salingar, Leo. "Crowd and Public in *Bartholomew Fair*." *Renaissance Drama*, n.s., 10 (1979): 141–59.

Sanders, Wilbur. *The Dramatist and the Received Idea*. Cambridge: Cambridge University Press, 1968.

Sargeaunt, M. Joan. *John Ford*. Oxford: Basil Blackwell, 1935.

Sasek, L. A. *The Literary Temper of the English Puritans*. Baton Rouge: Louisiana State University Press, 1961.

Schleiner, Louise. "Providential Improvisation in *Measure for Measure*." *PMLA* 97:2 (March 1982): 227–36.

Sensabaugh, G. F. *The Tragic Muse of John Ford*. 1944. Reprint, New York: Benjamin Blom, Inc., 1965.

Sharpe, Kevin. *Criticism and Compliment: The Politics of Literature in the England of Charles I*. Cambridge: Cambridge University Press, 1987.

―――. *The Personal Rule of Charles I*. New Haven: Yale University Press, 1992.

――― ed. *Faction and Parliament Essays on Early Stuart History*. Oxford: Oxford University Press, 1978; New York: Methuen, 1985.

Sharp, Kevin and Steven Zwicker, eds. *Politics of Discourse. The Literature and History of Seventeenth-Century England*. Berkeley: University of California Press, 1987.

Sinfield, Alan. *Faultlines: Cultural Materialism and the Politics of Dissident Readings*. Berkeley: University of California Press, 1992.

―――. *Literature in Protestant England, 1560–1660*. Totowa, New Jersey: Barnes and Noble, 1983.

Skura, Meredith. *The Literary Uses of Psychoanalysis*. New Haven: Yale University Press, 1981.

Smith, Warren D. "More Light on *Measure for Measure*." *Modern Language Quarterly* 23 (1962).

Smuts, R. Malcolm. *Court Culture and the Origins of a Royalist Tradition in Early Stuart England*. Philadelphia: University of Pennsylvania Press, 1987.

Snyder, Susan. "The Left Hand of God: Despair in Medieval and Renaissance Tradition." *Studies in the Renaissance* 12 (1965): 18–59.

Southall, Raymond. "*Measure for Measure* and the Protestant Ethic." *Essays in Criticism* 11 (1961): 10–33.

Spikes, Judith Doolin. "The Jacobean History Play and the Myth of the Elect Nation." *Renaissance Drama*, n.s., 8 (1977): 117–49.

Spinrad, Phoebe S. "*Measure for Measure* and the Art of Not Dying." *Texas Studies in Language and Literature* 26 (Spring 1984): 74–93.

Spivak, Bernard. *Shakespeare and the Allegory of Evil*. New York: Columbia University Press, 1958.

Stachniewski, John. *The Persecutory Imagination: English Puritanism and the Literature of Religious Despair*. Oxford: Oxford University Press, 1991.

Steane, J. B. *Marlowe: A Critical Study*. Cambridge: Cambridge University Press, 1965.

Stevenson, David. *The Achievement of Shakespeare's Measure forMeasure*. Ithaca: Cornell University Press, 1966.

Stevenson, Laura Caroline. *Praise and Paradox: Merchants and Craftsmen in Elizabethan Popular Literature*. Cambridge: Cambridge University Press, 1984.

Stone, Lawrence. *The Crisis of the Aristocracy, 1558–1641*. Oxford: Oxford University Press, 1967.

Stuart Royal Proclamations, edited by James F. Larkin and Paul L. Hughes. Oxford: Clarendon Press, 1973.

Sturgess, Keith. *Jacobean Private Theatre*. New York: Routledge Kegan Paul, 1987.

Teague, Frances. *The Curious History of Bartholomew Fair*. Lewisburg: Bucknell University Press, 1985.

Tennenhouse, Leonard. *Power on Display: The Politics of Shakespeare's Genres*. New York: Methuen, 1986.

The Thirty-nine Articles of the Church of England, ed. Edgar C. S. Gibson. London, 1897.

Thomas, P. W. "Two Cultures? Court and Country Under Charles I." In *The Origins of the English Civil War*, edited by Conrad Russell. New York: Harper and Row, 1973.

Thompson, Elbert N.S. *The Controversy Between Puritans and the Stage*. New Haven: Yale University Press, 1903.

Tricomi, Albert H. *Anticourt Drama in England, 1603–1642*. Charlottesville: University Press of Virginia, 1989.

Tyacke, Nicholas. *Anti-Calvinists: The Rise of Arminianism*. Oxford: Clarendon Press, 1987.

———. "Puritanism, Arminianism, and the Counter Revolution." In *The Origins of the English Civil War*, edited by Conrad Russell. New York: Harper and Row, 1973.

Urry, William. *Christopher Marlowe and Canterbury*. Boston: Faber and Faber, 1988.

Waith, Eugene. "John Ford and the Final Exaltation of Love." In *Patterns and Perspectives in English Renaissance Drama*, edited by Eugene Waith. Newark: University of Delaware Press, 1988.

Wasson, John. "The Secular Saint Plays of the Elizabethan Era." In *The Saint Play in Medieval Europe*, edited by Clifford Davidson. Kalamazoo: Western Michigan University, Medieval Institute Publications, 1986.

Wedgwood, C. V. *Poetry and Politics Under the Stuarts*. Cambridge: Cambridge University Press, 1964.

———. *Seventeenth Century English Literature*. 2d ed. New York: Oxford University Press, 1970.

———. *The Thirty Years War*. London: Jonathan Cape, 1938.

Wells, Henry. *Elizabethan and Jacobean Playwrights*. New York: Columbia University Press, 1939.

West, Robert H. "The Impatient Magic of *Dr. Faustus*." *English Literary Renaissance* 4:2 (Spring 1974): 218–40.

White, Paul Whitefield. *Theatre and Reformation: Protestantism, Patronage, and Playing in Tudor England*. Cambridge: Cambridge University Press, 1993.

Wilks, John S. *The Idea of Conscience in Renaissance Tragedy*. New York: Routledge, 1990.

Willson, David Harris. *King James VI and I*. New York: Oxford University Press, 1956.

Wilson, C. *England's Apprenticeship, 1603–1763*. 2d ed. New York: Longman, 1984.

————. *Seventeenth-Century English Literature*. New York: Oxford University Press, 1970.

Winwood, Sir Ralph. *Memorials of Affairs of State in the Reigns of Queen Elizabeth and King James*. Edited by Edmund Sawyer. 3 vols. London, 1725.

Wright, Louis B. *Middle-Class Culture in Elizabethan England*. Chapel Hill: University of North Carolina Press, 1935.

Wymer, Roland. *Suicide and Despair in the Jacobean Drama*. New York: St. Martin's Press, 1986.

Yachnin, Paul. "The Powerless Theater." *English Literary Renaissance* 21 (Winter 1991): 49–74.

Editions of Plays

Ford, John. *The Chronicle History of Perkin Warbeck*. Edited by Peter Ure. Manchester: Manchester University Press, 1968.

————. *Perkin Warbeck*. Edited by Donald K. Anderson, Jr. Lincoln: University of Nebraska Press, 1965.

Heywood, Thomas. *If You Know Not Me You Know Nobody*. Edited by Madeleine Doran. Oxford University Press, The Malone Society, 1935.

Jonson, Ben. *Bartholomew Fair*. Edited by Eugene Waith. *The Yale Ben Jonson*, Alvin Kernan and Richard B. Young, General Editors. New Haven: Yale University Press, 1963.

————. *Works*. Vol. 10, edited by C. H. Hereford and Percy and Evelyn Simpson. Oxford: Clarendon Press, 11 volumes, 1952.

Marlowe, Christopher. *Doctor Faustus*. Edited by Roma Gill. London: A and C Black, 1985.

————. *Doctor Faustus, 1604–1616*. Edited by W.W. Greg. Oxford: Clarendon Press, 1950.

————. *Doctor Faustus: A 1604-Version Edition*. Edited by Michael Keefer. Lewiston, New York: Broadview Press, 1991.

Massinger, Philip. *The Plays and Poems of Phillip Massinger*. Edited by Philip Edwards and Colin Gibson. Oxford: Clarendon Press, 1976.

Rowley, Samuel. *When You See Me You Know Me*. Edited by F.P. Wilson. Oxford University Press, The Malone Society, 1952.

Shakespeare, William. *Measure for Measure*. Edited by J.W. Lever. New York: Random House, 1965.

Index